Claire Guest

'Listened to Daisy'

Claire Guest
"Listened to Daisy"

This book is dedicated to my family -
Mum, Dad, sisters Louise, Nicole and Simone
and to all the special dogs in my life who have taught me so much
especially Woody who taught me never to give up!
***

Compiled & Edited by Terry Gasking, TwigBooks
Cover by Rebecca Slough, D5 Design
Photography Janine Warwick and others
The views expressed in the text are those of the author and should not be taken as representing those of any other person, institute, or organisation.

Claire Guest
"Listened to Daisy"
First published in 2014 by TwigBooks
Paperback ISBN 978-1-907953-57-6

Download into your iPad, Tablet or Computer in full colour from
www.twigbooks.com
Also available from Medical Detection Dogs : 01296 655888
www.medicaldetectiondogs.org.uk
and Amazon, EBooks, Kindle

TwigBooks
1-2 Biggs Lane, DINTON, Aylesbury, Buckinghamshire
UK, England HP17 8UH
www.twigbooks.com

Dr Claire Guest BSc (Hons) MSc DSc

Claire showed an incredible affinity to dogs from the time she struggled to get out of her pushchair and embrace every dog she saw. An affinity that was to last through her research at University, her work with Assistance Dogs and on through her lifetime. Claire has become renowned as one of the world's leading dog trainers and behaviourists. Her observation and knowledge of dogs convinced her that dogs could sniff out cancer and other life threatening diseases.

Despite the scepticism of much of the medical establishment Claire Guest was determined to prove her theories and she has done so spectacularly well. With a few fellow enthusiasts she set up the charity 'Medical Detection Dogs' in 2004 and by 2014 has more than 60 dogs out with owners proving their case. Daisy – her beautiful Labrador has rapidly established a worldwide reputation for identifying cancer from urine samples and obtains results that astound. In 2014 a newspaper headlined her as *'Daisy the dog who has sniffed out 500 cases of cancer'*

This is a fascinating book that takes us from Claire's life as a country girl in the beautiful countryside of Dorset, England, through the traumas of school, then losing her beloved pets, husband and nearly her sanity as she battled severe stress and depression to huge success with her dogs and her Charity – Medical Detection Dogs.

Working in a Vet's practice in Swansea whilst studying at University and influenced by one of Britain's leading dog behaviourists she became determined to prove that if you listened to your pets they will use their unique attributes to help you.

She listened to Daisy who diagnosed cancer in Claire and provides immensely accurate diagnosis from urine samples of people unknown to her. Dogs trained by Claire Guest hugely improve the quality of life for so many people with life-threatening health problems. They get their insulin or sugar needs for them even before they know that an attack is imminent. Their actions save lives.

This is a fascinating book that gives an insight to Claire Guest, her beliefs, the battle she had to gain acceptance of her ideas and highs and lows of her life and of many of the dogs she has trained and loved.

Claire Guest
"Listened to Daisy"

Contents

***

Claire Guest
"Listened to Daisy"

Illustrations

Claire Guest
"Listened to Daisy"

Chapter One
Schooldays

For some completely unknown reason I had an amazing affinity to dogs almost from birth. I would rock and struggle to get out of my pushchair to embrace every dog I saw. My parents tell me that I adored all dogs but particularly a Dalmatian that the family passed on their way to church. We did not have any animal at home so they had no explanation of where this deep love of dogs had come from.

I wouldn't let my parents pass 'Spotty Dog' as I called the Dalmatian without me screaming with excitement. Mum and Dad felt sufficiently moved to buy me a stuffed toy in the colours of a Dalmatian. The toy was immediately named 'Spotty' and I still have it today, When its stuffing falls out I push it back in and though it is over 40 years old it still occupies pride of place in my bedroom.

Since I could walk I had cuddled every dog I saw. Along the way a few had bitten me so my parents felt it would be wise for the family to get a dog in the hopes that I could learn to manage my emotions whenever a dog was in the vicinity

Thus 'Angel' a Pyrenean Mountain Dog became our first dog but sadly she was no 'angel'.

She had a suspected tumour that affected her temperament badly and didn't live very long. Her poor behaviour and untimely death upset us all.

Much later in my young life when I moved with my family away from all the animals I loved my parents, after constant pestering by me, thought it wise for me to have another dog. We went to a rescue centre and rescued 'Liza' a Labrador. Liza lived with us for 14 years but we had soon

discovered why she was in the rescue centre. They had told us that Liza was very protective of the family but had wanderlust. If she was taken for a walk by someone who wasn't particularly doggy she would bite the lead out of their hand, take off and not be seen for hours.

Liza was not the ideal dog for the budding Dog Trainer, but then again – perhaps she was!

On one occasion the local Irish Priest came to call on us. I opened the door and out shot Liza to protect us. The priest was last seen hurtling up the drive and into his car. Unfortunately in his haste he got his head caught on a hanging basket as he scrambled in the car. He managed to refrain from any unpriestly language was heard muttering *"There is no hole in your bucket dear Liza"*

Eventually the family and I managed to train Liza and I learned a great deal of how to manage a difficult dog. Liza was to go on and live happily with us for 14 years.

It was to be more than 20 years later before 'Daisy' entered my life. In those intervening years I was to know and love some wonderful dogs, ponies and horses and get to know many hundreds of dogs.

But all of this was in the future as Claire Guest emerged into this world.

I was born in Sedgeley near Dudley in the industrial heart of middle-England but soon moved to Winchester where we had a dog next door. It was a corgi and I got bitten by it regularly as I tried to give it a cuddle. Strangely my parents never banned me from seeing the corgi despite the teeth marks he left in me and he did teach me my first lesson in respect.

It was clear that I loved dogs and without one in my own house I decided to run away from home.

I took my toy dog Spotty and a pint of milk that was on the doorstep and turned up on my neighbour's door saying that I had run away from home and come to stay with her and her dog. I was 4 years old.

Our neighbour said that I couldn't stay with her but I could in future go with her daughter when she took the dog for a walk.

That settled me down and I was reasonably content until we moved to Dorset a year or so later.

When we were in Winchester my parents had put me into a Convent Nursery where the Nuns were very strict and unyielding. They were very fierce. They constantly told us children off for anything that happened.

On one occasion I was in a lunch queue when the boy in front of me vomited all over the place without any prior warning. For some reason the Sister in charge decided it was my fault and started blaming me.

I was only 4 years old but clearly remember how impossible it was to get her to accept that I had no way of knowing that the lad was going to be sick. It was one of my very early lessons in life that sometimes things can be incredibly unfair and people will pursue their own way irrespective of whether it was right or wrong.

I told my parents hoping they might be able to get a more just reaction but as we were about to move to Dorchester in Dorset they let it rest. In Dorchester I attended another Catholic School.

My parents and Grandparents were all very strong Catholics so it was natural that they would wish for their daughter/granddaughter to be educated in Catholic Schools.

My Granddad had originally been Church of England but wanted to marry my Grandmother who came from a staunchly Catholic family. My Great-grandfather was very unhappy with his son marrying someone from outside their faith and banished my Grandfather to Canada.

He was sent off with virtually nothing. Just enough cash to buy a saddle so Granddad became a cowboy on the Canadian Prairie. He was hired on a yearly basis at the Calvary Stampede but then caught TB and he was nursed back to health at a convent in Canada where he converted to Catholicism and came back and married my Grand-mother.

In Dorchester my mother started to give birth to a number of girls and though I was delighted to have younger sisters I longed for a 'spotty' dog but there was no time or inclination for my parents to acquire animals in the home.

Dad's job was in the management of local councils and he kept moving up a rung or two each time he moved to another local authority.

We went with him each time. From Sedgeley to Winchester to Dorchester to Weymouth to Winterbourne Houghton near Blandford Forum all before I was 12 years old.

Each time I was moved away from my young friends and tried to make new but I was intensely shy and this always proved to be exceedingly difficult for me. However, at Weymouth a life changing moment arrived - I joined a local riding school.

I had gazed at ponies in fields around our area and longed to groom and ride them. Now for the first time this was possible and I was very excited.

I wanted to go up and help evenings and at weekends. I helped muck-out and soon developed a strong relationship with the ponies and horses. 'Peanuts' the New Forest pony who used to buck everybody off, a little Shetland pony 'Champion' were my favourites. Anytime I could get a lift to the stables I would be there. Although I was very young I longed to take a pony over the jumps.

At Weymouth my sisters and I had been given Space Hoppers. A Space Hopper was a toy that was very popular in the 1970s. It consisted of a large spongy ball about 2 feet across that had two 'ears' sticking up. The skill was for the child to sit on the ball, hold onto the ears and then bounce his/her way across the ground.

It was great fun for a youngster who could pretend that the Space Hopper was a pony, or even a show jumper jumping all the small barriers I would have put up around the garden. My sisters got involved and we started racing our space hoppers. We erected a number of massive jumps on the 'space hopper show jumping course' we constructed and we jumped anything in our way, garden brooms, rakes, buckets, rubble. We were constantly puncturing our space hoppers and I became an expert at repairing them, often taking in any of our friends 'injured' rides and repairing them. No wonder I wanted to be a vet.

I made my own stables for the Space Hoppers. Each had its own little stable and every night it was my sisters and my job to go and check the stables and make sure the Space Hoppers had enough imaginary hay, water and were bedded down alright. I was thrilled to learn that the school we had enrolled in had a Space Hopper race as part of its sports day but devastated to be ruled too old to compete. My younger sister Louise could compete and after all our fun we had through our Space Hopper 'show jumping' competitions she won by a mile – to huge family pride.

Space Hopper was a great toy that gave the young Claire Guest years of enjoyment. However - the one that really took my breath away came one Christmas when Father Christmas had brought me a toy riding school. It was all soft plastic but it had everything you could want in it. Horses, saddles, a ménage, show jumps, stables, everything! I absolutely loved it.

Whenever I wasn't out on my bike or on my Space Hoppers I was playing with this riding school. I've still got bits of it now.

Riding became my passion. Helping at the stables and learning the correct way to ride. I was taught by a schoolmarm type woman who insisted we did everything absolutely correctly. She would not tolerate any other way. If you were in charge of that horse you held onto the halter come what may, you never let go of it. You were responsible for that horse and woe betide you if it got loose and disturbed anyone else or any other horse or animal. You never ever left a gate open, and so on.

I am so grateful to her and all the other people who taught helped and guided me in my early years at the riding school. It was wonderful training for anyone who was to spend time around horses. If I hadn't had such training I would never have developed such a  love and understanding of the countryside or been able to mix with the people I came to know.

In those days the riding position was much different from today. Then we used to ride hunt style. You stick your legs out and sit back in the saddle, now we keep our centre of gravity deep down into our legs so I had to relearn my riding style much later in life.

I loved the life at the stables but my enjoyment of my life generally was blunted because I was always very shy. I wouldn't answer the phone at home or anywhere else and I was very shy with people but never with animals who I continued to embrace wholeheartedly.

Claire Guest
"Listened to Daisy"

To help me overcome my shyness my Mum and Dad sent me away to a guide camp but for me it was a disaster. I was desperately homesick and I wanted to go home all the time.

Dad was always very busy with his career at which he would work away on occasions. When working at home he would work into the night if necessary.

Mum and Dad had made an agreement with each other - which of us girls they got up to look after in the night if they were wanted. My Dad chose me as I was oldest he thought he would get up less but he drew the short straw! I got him up every single night until I was about 9 years old. I used to suffer badly from nightmares.

On one occasion when Dad was working away from home from Monday to Friday I was watching the film 'The Railway Children' and became distraught. I became convinced that he was in prison as was the father in the film. My Dad came home as usual that Friday evening and the relief I felt when I saw him in the doorway has stayed with me all my life.

At that time I was about eight and a half years old and my parents thought it a good idea if we got a puppy and I learned to look after it properly.

We went to a rescue centre and 'Angel' a Pyrenean Mountain dog became our first dog. We chose her as a puppy but as I recorded earlier she was no 'angel'.

She had a suspected tumour that affected her temperament badly and didn't live very long. Her poor behaviour and untimely death upset us all. We had loved her and tried to do all the right things. We had researched the breed but her medical condition was too much for her to cope with. We were so sad when her life ended prematurely.

We had moved to Winterbourne Houghton near Milton Abbas in a most beautiful part of Dorset. Dad had worked extremely hard and had become the Chief Executive Officer of the North Dorset District Council and we were able to purchase a lovely cottage in this quiet village.

It was a village with one general store/post office and a couple of hundred cottages. Our cottage was in a small lane and backed onto fields. The field on the opposite side of a lane that was only about 10 yards wide was ideal for a pony of my own and I used to dream of such an occurrence.

The whole village was peaceful and idyllic but I had to leave the friends I had made in Weymouth behind and start again. However, my acute shyness made it difficult to make new friends and the change of school to Blandford High – a Comprehensive School - increased that difficulty.

The pupils at the school had difficulty in accepting this gangly, thin newcomer amongst them. They had all been together during primary school from 5 years old and now at the comprehensive came this shy diffident girl with a different accent that they considered to be 'posh'.

To make matters worse they discovered that my father was the Chief Executive Officer of Dorset District Council and therefore regarded me as one of the toffs and not one of them.

My interests were animals and the countryside and I longed for a pony to ride and look after. To the 'toughies' at school this was behaviour that was far from their ways and with an accent that was also clearly different from theirs. This girl who had previously been educated at 'Private Schools' – be they Catholic convent schools - was clearly not one with them.

As always, when someone treads a path that is not in accord with a dominant group of people a kind of reverse snobbery takes over and the group can become very intolerant of that individual. In the worst cases that occur all too often the 'mobs' behaviour can turn aggressive or even violent for no real reason. So it was at Blandford Comprehensive School and the behaviour of many of the other children soon deteriorated until every day the school turned into a chamber of horrors for me.

The village we lived in was lovely but there was no riding school and I had not made any friends but one day there was a knock on our door and this lady was on the doorstep. She was dressed like and looked to me like a witch. She looked very old; I cowered away but heard her ask Mum

'Does your daughter ride horses?'

'Yes she does'

'Well I have two horses and a pony called Belle and I wondered if your daughter would be interested in riding her'

What a wonderful offer!

Belle effectively became my pony. I rode her at Pony Club events and gymkhanas and learned how to jump on this brave pony. My passion soon became jumping and I would jump Belle over every obstacle I could find. I loved it and would jump anything.

Belle was 14.2 hands high so nearly the size of a horse and would tackle any fence or obstacle I put her to.

I started entering all the show jumping, pony club and gymkhanas that I could get to.

I was lucky because within a short distance was Higher Houghton which was the centre for all the Pony Club events in our area. It was very rare we needed to go anywhere else. When such an occasion occurred I would cadge a lift from anyone with room to spare in a horse box.

At this point I met up with Lady Alice Douglas. Lady Alice was the daughter of the Marquis of Queensbury and she had quite an eventful life. Many years later she was doing Drama in prison as a prison visitor when she fell in love with one of the prisoners and married him.

As a child she was a lovely friend and as nutty as a fruitcake in the loveliest of ways. She had a pony called Sweetie and we used to ride together her on Sweetie – me on Belle.

She lived in a house that had been split off from the estate of the Marquis and at week-ends and during holidays I used to stay with her at her house. It was up-market from ours but extremely homely.

I remember her Mum deciding one day that we would have Apple Pie for pudding and Alice saying –

'Come on we'll go and scrump the apples'

16

This really caught me out, I was terrified for I was brought up and educated as a strict catholic and could not imagine stealing somebody's apples even though they were all falling to the ground and otherwise wasted.

Alice had no such compulsions and it was soon *'come on then give me a leg up'* and the two of us were over the wall and picking enough apples for the evening meal.

Unfortunately Alice and I have lost touch but during our teens we used to go off on mad rides mostly at the full gallop and leaping anything that got in our way. We would gallop everywhere and return covered in mud and deliriously happy. In holiday time we would go off all day with a packed lunch and not be seen until darkness was falling.

We had a freedom that is totally missing in the childhood of so many of the children today. In summertime we would go off to Pony Club camp and try every obstacle and challenge there was.

Mrs Halahan who was the owner of Belle and who I had taken to be a witch on our first meeting used to live in a house called Foxearth – a little flint cottage that looked across a valley to the chalk hills opposite. To me it was heaven on earth. I love chalk hills as these were the happiest days of my life.

The cottage got its name from a foxearth in her garden. Mrs Halahan knew every foxearth and badger sett in the area. When we used to go riding she would point them out to me, name the birds that were flying overhead, point out the animal's footprints and name the animal that had made them. She showed me everything she knew about the wildlife and told me how to care for it and live alongside it.

It was heaven for the animal lover that was young Claire. The only thing I was scared of was the herd of geese she had. They would not only squawk to alert that there were unexpected visitors but they would attack, in a truly frightening thing. When I cycled up I would try to distract them as I pedalled through them as fast as I could to get to the stables but if one of the two dominant males was there I didn't dare take them on.

Sadly my pony Belle started to age and I managed to persuade Mum and Dad that I should have my own pony. We couldn't afford to buy one but we were lucky to find an owner who was no longer riding and happy to loan the pony to me as long as I fed and looked after her.

So 'Galah' came into my life.

She was a dream come true; 14.3 hands high half Arab, half Polo Pony. I couldn't believe this beautiful horse was being given to me with Dad having an option to buy at some time in the future for a nominal fee. A chestnut with an Arab face and curled tale. She was absolutely beautiful.

The owners did warn us that she could be a bit unpredictable! When she arrived I couldn't wait to ride her. I duly tacked up and got on Galah for my first ride and promptly got thrown off straight away. After three attempts all of which immediately finished with me on the ground I realised that I needed to change my approach and eventually she let me on.

My much loved Nanna was with us the day Galah arrived. She had told me when I was a very young child -

'Claire, always remember you have a Guardian Angel and one day you may need to ask for help so never forget she is there. She is always there.'

I didn't understand the significance of her remark then but many years later I realised how prophetic she had been.

My mind was on my new horse. Galah and I absolutely loved each other.

She became the most loyal and brilliant horse but everyone else was terrified of her as she was quite mad. She hadn't been taught to jump properly and because she was an Arab she failed to tuck herself up tight to get all her power in her stride as she approached a jump.

Arabs are not natural at that and it is one of the reasons they seldom make good show jumpers. They can however be very fast across the ground and Galah used to get over fences by going full speed at them. To me this was terrific fun but it used to terrify the wits out of the other parents sitting around the showjumping ring at competitions.

My Dad tells a lovely story of one event on a nice sunny afternoon where the showjumping ring was surrounded by relatives and friends of the riders. The spectators all had picnics on little portable tables or on trays on their laps as they watched the riders neatly thread their way over the obstacles.

Then on came Claire Guest on Galah. The horse gathered up almost snorting and pawing the ground as it waited for the bell to signal that Claire could start. The bell started and off went Galah like a bat out of hell, sailed over the first fence at top speed whereby it looked as though we couldn't possibly stop or turn before we were into the crowd on the far side of the ring. Dad said there were picnic tables and trays going in all directions, people picked up what they could of their picnics and ran as they scrambled to get out of the way of this mad stampede of Galah and Claire only for me to be just able to turn Galah when almost up to the rope. Then off we set off at a mad gallop in the direction of the next fence soared over it and hurtled straight toward the people who were sat eating their picnics at the other side of the ring. Pandemonium resulted as picnics were scattered in all directions as the spectators scrambled out of the horse's presumed path. Again I was able to turn Galah when we were nearly on the rope and off we went at breakneck speed to the next fence. This went on as we cleared every fence and also cleared the spectators to a distance of at least 10 yards away from the ropes.

I left the ring with a clear round and completely unaware of the mayhem we had caused or the shattered nerves of all the watchers. I always had a lot of pride as I collected my clear round rosette.

This was Galah's way of competing in all events and in hacking over the countryside. Hacking for Galah and I was not at a pace normal to hacking but was at breakneck speed over every obstacle we could find.

I loved it even though it was difficult to get placed in event jump offs for the other competitors horses were tucked up and turning in mid-air as they confronted the next obstacle. Galah and I were 10 yards down the track before she could be turned.

We did manage to finish a lot of events with a rosette despite our speed and all the rosettes would come home with me and to be pinned up on the beam that ran across my bedroom. Every rosette told a story for me. To this teenage girl winning a rosette was like getting the crown jewels. Galah and I went everywhere together, taking on the biggest obstacles we could find.

My time out of school was heavenly but my school days were as horrible as it was possible to be.

I had taken my 11+ exams at Weymouth when I was attending St Augustine Catholic School. The exam was compulsory across the country to every 11 to 12 year-old in education at that time. The children that passed were considered able enough to go onto be educated at Grammar Schools where they would study for 6 to 8 'O' Levels when about 16 years old and 'A' Levels 2 years later.

Those who failed to pass the 11+ went on to be educated at secondary modern schools where the education was less intense academically but still they had the opportunity to take 'O' Levels. Some were offered a more technical education at Technical Colleges.

In the 1970s the county education authorities were encouraged to disperse with these different categories and roll all standards of pupils into one type of school known as a 'Comprehensive'.

Claire Guest
"Listened to Daisy"

When we moved to Winterbourne Houghton near Milton Abbas the only option for me was Blandford High – a comprehensive school. I was one of the few pupils who had passed the 11+. I was also one that had not gone through Primary School with all the others and was deemed to have a 'posh' accent having in my younger years gone to 'posh' schools.

I was later to ride horses at weekends, take part in Pony Club events, mix with and become good friends with the likes of Lady Alice and the 'horsey set', and I competed in athletics for Dorset in the long jump and hurdles.

I came to dread the school bus as it arrived each morning. As soon as I got on the bullies would be onto me, pulling my hair, physically assaulting me, taking my bag and stealing anything in it that took their fancy. It was truly awful and it would take place every day and continue on into school and the playground.

It was absolutely horrendous. I couldn't go anywhere in school without being bullied. I was hit, I was punched, I was shut into places, I was tall but extremely thin, there was no way I could fight back against them.

Being brought up in a catholic school the nuns had taught me to always be polite and non-aggressive. I had no way of knowing how to overcome the bullying and the thugs that perpetrated it.

Mum and Dad noticed my character beginning to deteriorate as I tried to gain acceptance by the group I was forced to mix with at school. I didn't want to be the 'Posh kid' anymore.

'Don't you talk posh!'
'You've got 2 cars'
'Your Dad drives around in a sports car'
'You go horse riding'
'You do the long-jump for Dorset'
'You're a Posh Kid'
'I'm going to push your face in!'

I would get beaten up for all of these reasons and any others my school 'mates' could think of.

I lived in repeated terror.

At about this time our Sports Master set out a load of hurdles across the running track.

I had been rushing at and leaping over barriers all my life; first on my Space Hopper imaginary ponies, then on my bikes leaping over anything I could find, then on real ponies and horses. Setting off at a gallop and leaping over hurdles was completely natural for me. Everyone else was tripping over the hurdles whereas I went flying down the track leaping over the hurdles and wondered what the bother was all about.

The teacher had been an athlete and recognised straight away that I was going to become a fast hurdler and hurtle down the long jump track to leap far further than my peers. He took me aside and got me practicing.

The hurdles were left out for me every day on the track and every lunch-time I would be out practicing. Pupils don't argue with the Sports Master so he effectively became a bit of a protector and I was able to practice without the fear of bullies. Sadly they still got at me on the way home on the coach. The bullying got even worse when Mum and Dad decided that I should learn to play a musical instrument. I did love music and it was to be a means of regaining my sanity in later life but the bullying and Blandford High was enough to kill the enthusiasm of anyone but the most dedicated enthusiast.

I wanted to play the flute or clarinet but sadly by the time I got to the music teacher those instruments had already been allocated to others and the only instrument left was the cello.

Can you imagine trying to get on a bus full of bullies with a cello case? They had it off me and tried to smash it to pieces. I dreaded them succeeding for I thought the music teacher would kill me if I turned up with a smashed cello. I came to hate the instrument and the screech I could get out of it.

If it hadn't been for week-ends when I could get away from it I just don't know what I would have done!!

None of my riding friends were at school with me, most were at private schools.

Claire Guest
"Listened to Daisy"

My Athletics was going well and in matches against other schools I was winning the long jump, high jump and the hurdles. We had some good boy athletes and they were winning their events so we were doing well as a school and becoming good friends in the process.

One day I came out of class and some of the bullies set on me in the playground however without me knowing my life was about to change for ever.

The bullying was spotted by two boys who were my fellow competitors in the school athletics team.

The athletes were terrifically fit and strong. They realised what was going on and descended on the bullies and gave them a really serious good hiding. They really belted them.

'If you or anyone else ever lays a finger on Claire Guest now or at any time in the future we will be back and smash you to pieces'

From that day on I became nearly untouchable. It was an end to being tied to trees, shut into cupboards and lockers in the changing room, being hauled over and into ditches, punched, assaulted and abused by the other pupils.

I gradually began to get the courage not only to look after myself but also to defend others who were being bullied. I was very fit from all my athletics and I was starting to develop into someone that you didn't mess with.

I hadn't realised how much the previous years of bullying had affected me until a boy living in my village started to help me mucking out my horse and just generally being around. He was being badly bullied at the same school. I decided to stand up for him and it worked until one day when his sister came along and said –

'He is madly in love with you. He has your name all over his books. He has a picture of you by his bed'.

I was shocked, immature, too young and certainly not up for that.

At 14 years old I had no interest in boys and certainly wasn't ready for that so very immaturely told him I wasn't interested in him and I dropped him.

I inadvertently made matters worse for him one day when I saw him being very badly bullied at school but as only a 14 year old can do I turned my head away and walked past ignoring him. I felt bad about it but I was sure it was the right thing to do. Six months later he committed suicide by hanging. I still have a severe conscience about the whole episode. It was to came back to haunt me many years later.

I had to pass the house he had lived in every time I walked down to the Post Office.

The Post Office was also a General Store and was the only shop in the village. It was run by an old lady and all her stock was ancient. My Mum used to send me down for some shopping and would say

'Whatever you do make sure you don't get her old stock.'

'How do I do that? She always gives me her old stuff'

'Well tell her you only want her new stock!'

The old lady would look at me and come up with this really old stuff and I would say to her-

'My Mum said that could I have some of your new stock'.

The old lady would give me a stare and then mutter away as she went back to the shelf to get her 'new' stock. Whether it was any newer than her 'old' stock we had no way of knowing but off I would go back home with my purchase.

We had a cat called Smokey and he used to follow me down to the Post Office and back just like a dog would. I loved that cat. He was a Burmese with a beautiful 'Smokey' grey coat and was a most beautiful cat.

Our village had almost no traffic passing through so Smokey could happily trot alongside or behind me whenever I walked around the village.

Claire Guest
"Listened to Daisy"

In 1976 the country suffered a huge drought followed by constant snow the following winter. The village got snowed in for nearly a month and they started to do helicopter drops for supplies. The roads were impassable so all the local horses were called to take their owners through the snow drifts to the next village where there were supplies.

I was so proud to be called to join them. Unfortunately my horse got the idea we were going hunting and in typical fashion with Claire Guest in the saddle saw every obstacle as a barrier to be jumped so we would go charging off and leap into deep snow where we needed to paddle our way out. This so disrupted the others that I was sent home in disgrace to my great embarrassment. It was a real 'Thelwell' moment.

As a teenager I was quite a tomboy and whether I would have ever developed strong maternal instincts is questionable. My feminine maternal instincts were not helped when as an 8 year old attending catholic school the nuns wheeled us into a class and without any preliminary warning sat us down to watch a video. It was a graphic portrayal of childbirth and it traumatised me giving me a deep fear of ever giving birth to a child.

The catholic schooling had left me feeling that anything remotely connected to sex was bad and the video and events in my time in hospital being treated for a recurrent tonsillitis definitely put an end to thoughts of giving birth long before they had a chance to form in the teenage Claire.

By the time I was 13 years old I had two sisters - Louise who was born when I was three and a half years old and think in retrospect that I rather resented that I had to share my Mum and Dad's love with her; and Nicole who was born when I was five and a half years old. By that time I had come to terms with having sisters to play with and had involved them in all the fun I had with space hoppers and my toy riding school.

We all had the same pocket money each week and I would go out and buy little horses for my toy riding school. Nicole never spent her pocket money but would build up piles of coins on the dressing table which she would then lend to me in the middle of each week when I had spent all my money. She then took it back with interest at our next pocket money payday.

Nicole would have a pile of money beside her and a little book where she worked out how much interest we had to pay her. She had it all under control and was only seven and a half years old. It is no surprise to any of us that she grew up to be a highly successful Investment Banker working in the City of London.

I had been kept well away from the birth of all my sisters as children were in those days. My abhorrence of childbirth since the video and the hospital and my wish not to have anything to do with babies was still with me and yet - when I was 13 and a half years old Simone - my third sister was born - and I absolutely adored her.

Mum had been quite ill so I helped look after my baby sister and did everything I could to help.

I had been really excited that she was going to be born, loved all the baby clothes that were appearing and I was so excited at her arrival. I couldn't wait to get home from school and help feed and change baby Simone. I did all I was allowed to do – taking her for walks in her pram, bathing and her feeding her – being taught to feed her properly, keeping an eye out for her. I became very much the older sister

It was all very strange for I still maintained the image that I was never going to have children

I was still loving my riding but sadly we sold Galah after a few years. With hindsight this was a mistake but I desperately wanted a horse that was better for jumping. By now I was very serious about my jumping so we got Cinzano - a pony that was a very good jumper, but I was never to develop such a good relationship with him as I had with Galah.

Cinzano had lived with other horses all his life so being alone in the field opposite home did not suit him at all. He became a complete escape artist. He used to get out of his field and roam the village at night eating other people's roses and trampling up their lawns. My Mum was mortified. Mum was never horsey and still goes around horses with some trepidation but she would get a phone call to tell her that my horse was in somebody's front garden and would she get it out! I'd be at school so she would have to collect this flipping pony that she rapidly came to dislike intensely..

However I did enjoy jumping events with Cinzano. He was a better competitor in that he didn't rush all over the place or approach the jumps at frantic speed. He did however have a bit of a mind of his own and if he got a bit bored he would suddenly swerve under an overhanging tree and brush his rider off.

I remember one occasion when Alice, my sister Louise and I had entered a more prestigious show. We spent hours grooming our horses at her house, polishing all the tack, dressing ourselves immaculately – hairnets, black jackets – Pony Club ties and so on. Riders and horses looked absolutely immaculate as we set off to the competition. We were watching a previous competitor go round the course when for some reason Cinzano got bored and went straight through a hedge. Off I came straight into thick mud. My hairnet was hanging from a branch in the hedge, my lovely tailored black jacket was covered in green slime and my beautifully polished riding boots were scratched all over. We were still able to compete but we looked a complete mess – another 'Thelwell' moment.

School was now very tolerable.

My days of being bullied were over. I was now a very formidable opponent if anyone wanted to take me on and I felt some satisfaction that I had been able to live through those years of horrendous bullying and come out the other side.

My new found confidence had allowed me to start to make friends of my own and Nikki and I became great friends doing everything together at school whilst Lady Alice and I were constant companions at week-ends and in the holidays.

I was competing at athletics for the school, running 75 metre hurdles in 12.3 which was the British qualifying time and I was running for Dorset. Unfortunately I had a nasty fall from my horse that left me with a back problem that was to last me for years until many years later when Nick Grove a physiotherapist in Wendover found a cure.

At 15 years old you hope the body can cope with it and life had become truly wonderful.

The comprehensive education was not too demanding and I could practice my hurdles, high jump and long jump every lunchtime. I got on well with the other members of the school athletics team and those at the county level. I had just been selected and run for England – what could be better?

I had begun to make good friends with many of my school mates and scholastic life was beginning to look very good. I competed in the long jump, high jump and hurdles for the school and the in the hurdles and long jump for Dorset. I had a qualifying time which was of National Standard and got called up to run for England against France.

Sadly my 'International' was one of my last really serious runs.

I had hurt my back when my pony fell and I took a nasty tumble. This along with my notorious slow start put me under a great deal of pressure. I tried to start as promptly as everybody else but would often jump the gun and be pulled back for a false start. The result was I stayed in my blocks until I was aware of the whole line of runners lifting as they started then off I would go – inevitably a few strides behind everyone else. This did not matter too much at school events or even county events for my speed over the ground and over the hurdles would soon close the gap, and I would usually manage to pass through the field to take the tape. At International level this was not so and the pressure my slow start put me under was destroying my confidence.

I had an UK National Vest but little satisfaction at my performance or my nerves going into the event.

I began to realise that my love of horses and my love of athletics might be in conflict with each other.

Claire Guest
"Listened to Daisy"

Out of school was heavenly. My pony wandered but Mum had the job of bringing it back to the field. At week-ends and in the holidays we were saddled up and competing at Pony Club events or riding for pleasure across the lovely countryside of Dorset.

One of the favourite rides of Lady Alice and I was up into the hills above Winterbourne Houghton. We could ride narrow bridleways and gallop madly across fields jumping every fallen tree, fallen branches and anything else we could find. It was bliss-full.

We would be in deep woods and come to a clearing where you could look down to the glorious views of Milton Abbey, the school and the lakes beyond. The route up Water Lane to a very narrow bridle path that went straight up the hill was incredibly beautiful. It was all flint and we would give the ponies a chance to stop so that we could check their shoes and make sure their feet were clear of flint or any other stones. At the top of the bridle path we came to three open fields that we would gallop across before dropping down the hills in the midst of glorious woodlands to Milton Abbas.

We could complete the ride in a couple of hours but we would spend our time jumping over any obstacle we could find and setting ourselves a race course through the twisting bridle paths where we would compete at top speed – eking out every ounce of speed from our ponies. We had our lunch sandwiches in our pockets and would give the ponies a rest while we sat under a tree and ate.

We had a number of routes we could take from here.

We would take in Higher Houghton, past Mrs Halahan's cottage, past the pony club's cross country course, Dullcott Wood, Cuckoo Lane, Milton Abbas, Lagden Copse – all free of traffic and only the sounds of the country around us.

I was just starting to appreciate the differences in the seasons and I loved them all. On one occasion even though we were some way from the coast a sea fog rolled in very quickly. We could see it rolling towards us and suddenly we were completely enveloped in thick fog. We had no idea which way we should go and some of our route was very narrow and precarious. Thank goodness we had the sense to rely on our ponies to get us home.

Ponies, horses and many other animals have an incredible sense of direction and a homing instinct. If you listen to them they will often guide you with unerring accuracy as they did on this particular day.

The variety of routes we could take meant we could ride for an hour, half a day, or dawn to dusk and we did so on every conceivable occasion in all weathers in all seasons.

Life could not be better.

I was deliriously happy. As a 15 year-old I thought that surely this happiness will go on for ever. How wrong I was!

I did not know it but my whole life was about to change completely

***

Claire Guest
"Listened to Daisy"

Chapter Two
My World Changes

'Dad and I have some really good news for you',
Mum and Dad were talking to me and my sisters.
'You know Daddy has been going up to Buckinghamshire and been interviewed for a much bigger job – well he has got it! Daddy is going to be the Chief Executive Officer of the Aylesbury Vale District Council. He will be one of the youngest CEOs in the country of any large council'.
I was delighted for both of them. They were obviously very happy with the news but what did it mean for us children?
'Well, we will be moving up to Aylesbury as soon as Daddy has found us a house and we will be living there.'
'But I don't know anything about Aylesbury!'
'Oh you will love it. It is the county town of Buckinghamshire and Buckinghamshire is a really attractive County. This is a really big step up for Daddy and we are all very proud of him'.
We moved. I was 15 years old and house prices were moving all over the place so Dad could not immediately find a house in or around Aylesbury that was suitable or that we could afford. I needed to start school in Aylesbury as my GCE 'O' Levels were only 12 months away so Dad, Louise and I lived in a caravan for 6 months; travelling up on a Monday early morning and back to Dorset on a Friday night.
I had always been a home lover and adored my family but now they and my lovely baby sister were left down in Dorset whilst I was spending Monday to Friday in a caravan in Aylesbury attending a school that had a number one priority of getting all its girls through their GCE exams to the exclusion of everything else. I hated it from the start.

Buckinghamshire might a very attractive county but its county town seemed to me to be hell on earth!

Aylesbury had once been a really lovely town full of little streets and lanes and centuries old houses and shops. Sometime after the war and before we arrived in the town the planners decided to rip the heart out of the town and build a 'modern' Aylesbury.

I had come from a life in the rolling chalk hills of lovely and peaceful Dorset where I walked across a narrow lane to greet my horse and where my beloved cat Smokey could walk to the Post Office and back with no sign of vehicles to threaten anybody's safety. There was peace and tranquillity and just the sounds of the country all around us.

Now I was in the middle of a town of wide roads, non-stop traffic and noise and surrounded by massive ugly buildings in the centre of which stood the 'Town Hall' – a multi-storied building that could be seen for miles around. Its shape and ugliness caused it to be known to the locals by a fitting but very rude name.

There was no sign of fields and woods and lovely chalk hills I had come to know and love and ride over throughout my summers.

There was nowhere to keep a horse so my pony was sold and to increase my despair and sorrow within days of us moving into a house in Aylesbury my lovely cat 'Smokey' got out one night and was run over and killed on the Oxford Road - the A418.

There was noise and pollution, and hustle and bustle, and wide roads full of traffic, and fumes, and drug users, with down-and-outs occupying the bus shelter with their smell of urine everywhere as they waved their bottle of meths. at any young girl who tried to catch a bus.

It was awful!

I could not believe I was supposed to live in this dreadful place. After the joys of Dorset surely life could now not get worse – but it could! I was enrolled at Aylesbury Girls High School at the start of the 4th form and scheduled to take my 'O' Levels at the end of that school year.

I had been bullied in Blandford as my accent was thought to be 'too posh' but now I was mocked for my Dorset accent as too backward. I was treated as a country bumpkin and I am certain some of the teachers thought of me as such even before they started teaching me.

I had been taught to a different curriculum in Dorset but now I was at a Grammar School where success in 'O' Levels and in 'A' Levels was everything and certain teachers seemed to think they were the 'bee's knees'.

Aylesbury Girls High!

They had an excellent record of high academic achievement whereas I had come from a school with comparatively low academic aspirations. I knew I would need to do a lot of work to catch up.

I had given the teachers at my new school all my work books from Dorset so they knew where I would be starting from on their curriculum.

Aylesbury Girls High School were very proud of their academic record and to 15 year-old me it seemed that everything was to be sacrificed in an attempt to achieve the best academic results possible for the school. I was not sure this was for the sake of the girls or for the sake of the status of the school.

At my interview the headmistress immediately informed me that there would be no time to be wasted on sport or country events. I was there to work for 'O' Levels and would need every minute of time available to catch up and stand any chance of passing.

How can I not continue my sport? I had just represented England at Athletics! I had an England qualifying time in hurdles and had competed for Dorset in hurdles, long jump and high jump and I was just 15 years old.

Claire Guest
"Listened to Daisy"

'You will find we do things differently here! If you are to take GCE 'O' Levels in a year's time you need every minute devoted to your studies.'

She was correct but I hated it!

I was to take English Literature, English Language, Geography, History, Maths, French, Biology, Chemistry, and a sub subject - Oral English.

I came to realise many years later that had my parents stayed in Dorset with the education available to me and not moved me to an academic based education I wouldn't have stood a chance in those examinations or in any that were to follow. Indeed my whole life would have been different from the one I have been privileged to live and I would never have been able to achieve all that I have.

However as a 15 year-old, with her animals sold and with her lovely Smokey run over and killed, I was not able to appreciate the wisdom of my parents move and I hated every day in this accursed town.

To make matters worse soon after starting at school I was called in by the Headmistress after I had been causing some commotion and she said –

'Claire – we are not snobs here [spoken in a tone and with body language that I took to mean the reverse of her words] *but you will find things very different from a mixed comprehensive'.* The last two words had been spoken as though she was disposing of a mouth full of trash.

'You are behind in every subject and unless you do better you have no chance in any of your 'O' Levels'

In class I was being mocked for my Dorset accent and for my Dorset ways and for the less strenuous education I had received at the only school that had previously been available to me. For some reason that I could not understand many of the teachers took a great delight in mocking and embarrassing me.

One day my English Teacher called me out to the front of the class.

Claire Guest
"Listened to Daisy"

'Girls,Girls I want you to look at Claire's feet.' Having got all their attention on my feet - *'Never, never in the whole of my life have I seen such an utterly scruffy pair of shoes!'* All said in the intonation that would have done Winston Churchill proud. She was a much fairer teacher than many and was passionate about her subject. I still keep in touch with her now but I always make sure I clean my shoes before we meet.

She may have had a point – I had been visiting a friend on a pig farm the previous weekend in those shoes but for the life of me I could not work out how this scorn was to help me pass my English exams.

Another day I was hauled up in front of the Head for walking along the passageway between the old part of the school and the new 6th form block.

It was a nice passageway – all carpeted and neat and tidy. If you didn't use the passageway then you had to go down a flight of stairs out of the door of the old part of the school round the end of it and back into a door on the new 6th form block and up a flight of stairs to re-join the other end of the passageway. The passageway did away with that need but for some unfathomable reason we girls were not allowed to use it and had to go outside and round when changing classrooms, even if it was pouring with rain.

This didn't make any sense whatsoever to me and one day when it was pouring with rain I walked the passageway.

That was it – up in front of the Head again.

'Claire, a rule is a rule, why does Claire Guest think she can break a rule? Why do you think we have this rule that students cannot walk along this passageway? I think you should give me some reasons why you think we have this rule then Claire Guest might learn to obey it. Give me some reasons why you think we have this rule.'

I didn't have a clue! The only thing I could think of was that they didn't want to wear the carpet out.

I thought this was a perfectly good answer but it was not the right answer. The right answer was that people using the passageway might disturb students working in the library that it ran alongside.

It still didn't make any sense to me.

The passageway was carpeted so it would have muffled the sound of the user's feet. A rule that forbade talking or making any extraneous noise in the passageway might have made sense but not one that sent all the students outside to get soaking wet when a passageway had been built to avoid that very situation.

Sadly my answer was not acceptable to the head and I was told I couldn't spend time on athletics as I needed to concentrate on my studies.

'You are so far behind in your studies that you will not be allowed to jump a hurdle until we can see that you have made a substantial improvement in your academic work'

For me this was a horrific decision.

I had just hurdled for England. Who knows what I might achieve? Now I was not being allowed to practice or take part in any athletic competition – not even matches against other schools.

I was not allowed to jump a single hurdle for months.

It was terrible and I thought it an awful life!

I had no animals – no athletics and I was desperately unhappy and resentful. I was horrified beyond all belief at the situation I was in at school, in Aylesbury, and at the way my life was working out without me having control over any of it.

Each morning Dad drove me the few miles to school and there in front of me was the horrible building dominating Aylesbury and seemingly my every step. What on earth was I doing here? What was happening to me?

I was so cross and angry and horrible that I was a nightmare for my parents. I could not wait to leave home and go back to the West Country that I loved.

Dad realised how desperate I was beginning to feel so despite the family not being doggy people, and the bad experiences we had with Angel - our only previous attempt to own a dog - we took ourselves to RSPCA rescue centre and 'rescued' a Labrador called Liza. She was lovely.

I still had an overwhelming desire to be a Vet even though I was told on my arrival at Aylesbury High.

'Ha, ha, you are never going to be a vet – you are never going to be a vet, you won't get to university! Why don't you be a secretary instead?'

But despite all they said I was still wanted to be a vet. Their continual disparity of my ambition and of me along with my anger at my existence in Aylesbury finally led to something inside me saying

'Stuff you Aylesbury, and stuff you teachers! I will do what I want to do in life. If it means working all hours then I will work all hours. I will do whatever is necessary to prove you wrong and do the things I want to do'.

I knew that I needed good 'O' Levels and 'A' Levels if I was ever to make it.

Despite an overwhelming desire to get away from this existence I knew my best chances of making it through these exams was through this awful school. I somehow would have to find a way of coping with the teachers who continually poured humiliation on my head. I had been severely bullied by the scary families at Blandford High and come through it successfully! I was not prepared to let a few bullying teachers at Aylesbury High deter me!

Once my exams were over then I would be off just as quickly as was possible.

Mum and Dad bought me all these books on 'How to pass your 'O' Level' and I worked on them every night in my bedroom accompanied by Radio Luxemburg.

I worked on my studies night after night thinking *'I will not let you rubbish me! I will not let you beat me down!'*

I sat 8 subjects and I passed 8 subjects.

Many years later I met my French teacher who told me

Claire Guest
"Listened to Daisy"

'Claire Guest you are the only person I have ever taught that I just cannot believe ever passed 'O' Level French! How you did it I will never know.'

It was the first time in my life that I realised that when pushed to despair a determination finally wells up within me that will not allow situations to dictate how I should react.

This determination to conquer the situation I found myself in was to prove a life-saver for me later in my life.

I was determined that I was not going to allow those teachers the satisfaction of saying that I was stupid. I was determined to bloody well prove them wrong. I will get 8 'O' Levels - and I did get 8 'O' Levels.

I eventually caught up on my studies and was allowed to jump hurdles on Sports Day.

All the parents turn up to watch, I was totally perplexed. How can you have a sports day when we haven't had any training?

I remember standing on the hurdles start line next to a girl who couldn't wait to tell me that *SHE* was the 'School Hurdler'.

The school had an athletics team that ran against other schools. I really wanted to be in the team and I would tell them that I used to run for Dorset.

'Yes we know all about that', would come the reply *'but you haven't time – you will stick to your studies'*

So I was never given a chance to show what I could do.

So now *'the school hurdler'* was alongside me in the line. The school were poor at sports – all their attention was getting the girls through as many subjects as possible in their 'O' Levels so their results came high up on any academic achievement tables anyone looked at.

The *'school hurdler'* was obviously one of the better athletes in the school. She looked at me and again said -

'You might have run for Dorset but I am the School's Hurdler and I have run 13.4!'

Everyone was looking at her in admiration as if to say *'Gosh she has run a 13.4'*

I never told her my best time.

The school had not allowed me to hurdle for the best part of a year. I had put up a course of bamboo canes in my back garden. It was only long enough for 3 hurdles but I jumped regularly. I didn't know what I would achieve in this race.

I didn't need any motivation to go flat out, the whole of my younger life trained me to always run flat out and fly over any obstacle that was put in front of me. I was the same on my space hopper, on my bikes, on my ponies, on Galah, and on the running track.

The *'School Hurdler's'* attitude and closing remarks showed that she didn't realise it but she was playing with fire.

'Yes I have a 13.4 so you won't be beating me!' she uttered just as we were about to start.

The race started and I flew down the track and over the hurdles. I breasted the tape as the winner - the *'School Hurdler'* was so far behind that she was still to jump the final hurdle.

That was a huge 'up yours' moment and I loved it. I've had quite a few more of these in my life since and all of them give immense satisfaction!

I was then allowed to do a little hurdling in the 6th form against other schools but much of the motivation had gone. I had come to realise that if I stayed at the school and concentrated on my studies I had a good chance of passing 'A' levels with high enough grades to get to University and maybe be a vet. Also I had now got another horse. It was named Wizard it was a Connemara thoroughbred, 15.3 hands high and lived in a field at Susan's House. Susan was a very good friend I had made at school. Wizard was with her horse out near Westcott, a village about 4 miles west of Aylesbury.

Westcott had a scattering of houses alongside a now disused wartime airfield. I say disused but at that time deep in the depths of the ground under the airfield they test-fired the rockets that carried Britain's Nuclear Missiles. We weren't to know that but every now and then there would be a massive crunch and the earth would literally shake as they test-fired a rocket for a few seconds. The vibrations in the earth could be felt many miles away but the horses did not seem to be at all put-out by it.

I wanted to spend as much time as I could with my horse but really only had week-ends. I had become good friends with Susan and we rode together across the countryside to the west of Aylesbury. It was not as beautiful as my beloved Dorset but I was beginning to find the Buckinghamshire was an attractive county. Whatever had it done to get such a dreadful county town?

I used to go with Susan to her home on Friday after school, stay with her and go back with her to school on Monday morning. My parents weren't seeing much of me but they were probably glad of that for I had become a very resolute young lady who knew her own mind and who was determined to pursue her own way of life.

I stayed most weekends with Susan and got a little of my old life back. It was not the same but was a massive improvement on that dreadful first year in Aylesbury.

Susan had a dog – a collie cross named Jack. I had my Labrador at home – Liza. Jack used to go riding with us. Susan's horse was very nervous in traffic so we would go across the bridle-paths, fields and hills. We didn't event or compete but the joy of riding was back with me.

It was here that my first boyfriend appeared in my life!

It was Susan's brother Richard. Richard was 21 years old and had an orange coloured Spitfire sports car that would speed us thrillingly around the countryside. I was 17 and we became very close. My love of going quickly has always stayed with me so we were speeding around the beautiful lanes of Buckinghamshire, and indeed speeding along in our relationship.

He was at Agricultural College in Devon and his family were country folk so when he was home on holiday or for week-ends I was back to a lifestyle of picking wild mushrooms in the fields, sloes from the trees, blackberries from the bushes and everything else we could gather from the countryside.

I had clawed back some of the country life I adored.

'A' Levels were still ahead. The set I was in at school had Geography, Biology and Chemistry instead of Physics, Biology and Chemistry that I needed if I was to become a Vet and as I got my results I began to realise that they were not good enough for me to make it as a vet.

My dreams of becoming a female 'James Herriot' were fast disappearing but I couldn't think of what else I wanted to do. I knew I had to work and have a life that was centred on animals

I had always been determined to leave Aylesbury as soon as I got my 'A' Levels but now I had the pull of my horse Wizard, my dog Liza, and boyfriend Richard to keep me there.

Susan's brother was a lovely first boyfriend. He was reliable, honest, moral, and loving. We loved walking together and had very close interests. We would pick mushrooms and be very aware of all the animals in the fields and the birds that were around us. Life with him as a boyfriend and my pony and dog as company took me back to that life I loved.

He was the eldest son of a farming family and was undemonstrative and steady. He used to find me a handful when I dragged him into local discos. I would be up as soon as the music started, dancing frenetically with body and arms flying all over the place. Richard would be next to me shifting his weight carefully from foot to foot. He was never more relieved that when his sister Susan went with us. He would sit quietly watching Susan and I dance like a couple of whirling dervishes.

Richard was undoubtedly very fond of me and even asked me to marry him. I did think about it seriously but wasn't ready to settle down. I wondered if Richard would be too steady for me.

At that time I began to get quite spiritual in many ways and had a growing belief that you really could make things happen if you believed deeply enough. Richard was unassertive kind and lovely but maybe could not fulfil the sense of adventure a teenage girl needed. I needed him to be more assertive and believe in himself much more. One evening we were walking in the fields and I was saying –

Claire Guest
"Listened to Daisy"

'Do you think that if you believe in something strongly enough you can make it happen?'

'No Claire, things happen – you can't always control them.'

'I don't mean you control them but I really do think that if you really believe something will happen then it will.'

'You do talk a lot of old rubbish at times Claire,

'No, I'm serious. Take those clouds that are above us. There are stars hidden above them. If you believe hard enough then the clouds will part and there will be a circle of stars directly over your head'

'Oh Claire, where on earth do you get this nonsense from?'

'No, listen, do it for me! Really believe me that if you look up and stare at the clouds they will part and you will see a circle of stars above your head. Please, please do it for me, but you must first believe that it really will happen.'

I had finally persuaded Richard to humour me but I made him really believe it was going to happen before letting him look upwards. Finally he stared up at the clouds overhead and a very strange thing happened. There came a break in the clouds and directly over my boyfriend's head was a circle of stars!

Richard became a committed Christian shortly after this episode.

His was a very moral family and I had a very committed Catholic upbringing so there was no thought of sleeping together even though we were born at the time of the swinging sixties. I became a part of the family and became incredibly fond of every one of them.

Richard was a lovely lad and we loved each other deeply.

My horse was stabled in the field behind his house and I spent my week-end with them so I used to spend a lot of time with him. Everyone, including me, somehow expected that we would marry and settle down together.

I was a teenage girl who longed for a bit of excitement and adventure rather than continuing the strict moral upbringing that had been with me all my life. I often think I should have married him but I was just 19 years old and like most girls of my age I wanted a bit more excitement in life, a bit of pizzazz, discos and doing mad things. These were not the ways of Richard.

Then, at the discos I met Steve.

He was in many ways the antithesis of my boyfriend. Steve was a whirlwind by comparison, - had a wicked naughty streak and would dance madly as Susan and I did. He would do things on the spur of the moment without fear of the results. Steve was a good lad who worked at a home with children who were mentally disabled and he was very good with these kids and very effective in his work.

Steve was very comfortable in himself. His immediacy of actions often with little or no forethought and all done with great verve and humour offered all the excitement and danger that had been missing in my very comfortable relationship with Richard.

My physical shape began to develop and I began to realise that I had grown out of the terribly thin gawky spotty girl into one that boys wanted to date. I had somehow thought that would never happen but it did and it opened the door to all kinds of adventures I had never imagined in my life before.

However I began to realise that my life needed more excitement and adventure in it than Richard could offer and Steve might well be the one who could provide it. Furthermore Steve had become obsessed with me.

He seemed to idolise the ground I walked on. Every morning he would run into Aylesbury to leave a red rose on my doorstep and this went on for a long time. My Dad was furious and really worried what effect Steve would have on the morals and behaviour of his daughter.

When I told my boyfriend Richard that things were over between us as I had met this other man I felt that I had let him down very badly. His family were devastated as were all who knew us. His sister – my really wonderful friend Susan - was so angry that she could hardly speak to me and it badly damaged our relationship. I started seeing Steve and going with him to every disco we could find.

Then my 'A' Level results came through and they were very disappointing.

Without 'A' grades my hopes of going to University were in jeopardy and my hopes of being a Vet were dashed. I did think of going to a college and trying for an 'A' in physics and maybe resurrecting my chances of being a vet. My hopes and aspirations had been dashed and I really didn't know which avenue to follow from here. What to do now?

There was a steady and loving Richard and his family that I had let down very badly by backing out of a relationship everyone expected to end in marriage.

'Could I restore their trust and settle down to domesticity with them?

There was a loving madcap adventurous Steve who offered insecurity but massive excitement.

I felt that I was in a deep dilemma.

Should I get away for a while and give myself time to think things through. Richard had achieved his agricultural degree and had sung the praises of the college he had attended in Devon. The college placed new students onto a farm in the lovely Devon countryside for the first year so that you absorbed a year's practical knowledge of farming before you started on the academic studies. If I went there it would at least put me out amongst the animals for a year.

Should this be the route for me?

I was still a home lover and loved my parents and my 3 sisters so perhaps I should settle down at home and *get a 'proper job' nine to five.* So should it be -

Richard?

Steve?

Physics course at College?

Try for University?

Agricultural College?

or a 'proper job' 9 – 5 in an office somewhere?

Claire Guest
"Listened to Daisy"

These were the choices that seemed to be facing 18/19 year-old Claire Guest. I knew they were all life changing journeys but which should I take?

What did I really want to do with my life, what did I believe in?

***

Chapter Three
Home Farm, Devon

Seale Hayne Agricultural College had been the college at which Richard had studied and it was in beautiful rolling countryside just outside Newton Abbot in Devon. The first year was activity year. You registered with the college and then went and spent the year on a farm – in my case it was to be Home Farm.

From my memory of Home Farm, Clyst St Lawrence it covered approximately 400 acres of the lovely Devon countryside. It had a herd of about 52 cows, chickens, farmyard animals and a couple of big horses that they used when out hunting. Their main crops were corn and hay, but they also grew potatoes, swedes, and similar crops and had some very productive apple orchards where the apples went to make the very strong scrumpy cider that is a speciality of the West Country. The farm was situated much closer to my beloved Dorset than the college at which I had enrolled.

It was a farm owned and run by a family and their son and daughter. Their eldest son had successfully got a Degree from Seale Hayne and had attended the College at the same time as Richard.

At this stage of my life I was suddenly finding that I was proving

to be attractive to boys and I was equally finding boys attractive. I certainly had eyes for David - the farmer's eldest son. He had fast cars and I was allowed to drive them and the tractor.

My pony Wizard had been sold and Liza

returned to my family so Claire Guest had arrived bag in hand and without animals to spend a year working on the farm.

They had not had any girls working there before my arrival and all the boys displayed a little of the attitude that they do the work whilst the girls baked the cakes and cleaned the house. However they were lovely people and I was soon the object for an incredible amount of good natured teasing.

They would have me at the top of the hay loft sorting the bales that they pitchforked up to me without telling me the location of the breathing spaces. I would fall a long way down these at regular intervals to the accompaniment of delighted laughter from all four of them.

My joy of driving was beginning to show itself and I was delighted when they allowed me to drive the tractor without supervision. At first they gave me simple jobs to do. muck-spreading was one. The cab of the tractor was simple plastic and before I learned that there was a back section to the cab they would set it up without it so as the tractor sprayed dung, muck and slurry in all directions it also soaked me from head to foot. So delighted was I to be allowed to drive I stuck at the task until it was complete and I could shower and get clean.

They played lots of tricks on me but each time I demanded that they show me how to do various tasks on the farm and they always did so my knowledge of farming was growing very quickly.

I soon became part of the team. When they ploughed or harvested I was driving a tractor. I was also good when driving the corn trailer truck that moved alongside and at the same pace as the combine harvester as it tipped the grain into my trailer.

Within that year I tackled everything on the farm including bailing. The only thing I was poor at was milking the cows. It was not because of my lack of technique but was because I am terrible at getting up in the morning so the cows would be milked before I got to the barn.

I would help rear calves and chickens and then I started riding the horses. The next door farm had a few hunters that I would ride. I was getting on very well with Dave and we had a very easy relationship

David and I were beginning to get quite close. We were living in his parent's house. It was a very moral family and my only doubts about my relationship with David was I thought he might be lacking ambition We both loved music and would listen to records together at the end of our long days working on the farm. I particularly remember the sunny days, the red deer and the quiet peaceful countryside.

I had a room of my own on the farm and when David and I started going out together Steve back in Aylesbury became very upset. Richard was by now no longer in my life.

David as eldest son would inherit the farm and I began to think that being a farmer's wife may not be such a bad life. I would be around animals even though much of my time might be sent getting them ready to be sold or taken to market.

I completed my year at Home Farm and then moved into Seale Hayne College. I was beginning to have doubts as to whether I had made the right choice in trying for an agricultural degree. My year on the farm had made me realise that that life followed an annual pattern, planting and feeding the fields early in the year, gathering and storing the harvest, and the part that haunted me very night as I tried to sleep – taking the calves away from their mothers as soon as the cows had come into milk.

Amongst all the calves that had been born that year we had the

most gorgeous calf but its mother was really deeply distressed when almost immediately after birth we took the calf away from her.

The mother called for her calf – pleading for its return non-stop all night and all through the following days. You couldn't help but feel her deep distress. I pleaded with David and the family to return the calf to its mother but they couldn't understand my concern.

'Don't be silly Claire! We can't do that. How do you think we get milk? The milk you drink on your cornflakes and drink in your tea comes from the cows that we have taken the calves away from, that's how you get milk!'.

It still appalled me. *'But the mother is so distressed! You can't just take her calf away from her. Listen to her – she is deeply distressed. You just can't do it, it's inhumane. There must be a better way!'*

'There isn't Claire. This is the way we have produced milk for hundreds of years, and we will go on producing milk this way for many more hundreds of years'

I was hand rearing some of these calves to supplement or compensate for the loss of their mother's milk or if they had "scours" due to the use of the artificial milk and their poor immunity. Sometimes they would die. It seemed to me a sad situation that calves were dying on artificial milk whilst their mothers were crying out for them.

It really made me question if a life in agriculture was the best option for Claire Guest; I even wondered if I could change the traditional ways of agriculture and improve the welfare of the animals!

So I started college in an unhappy state of mind with the immensely sad bleating of the cow constantly in my mind.

Within my first week in the college a bloke got into my bedroom. Thankfully I was able to rebuff him but the situation gave me an excuse that I think I was secretly looking for to back out of the agricultural degree.

I did consider whether I personally could change agriculture or whether I could work with animal charities but I could see no way of changing the practices I had seen but these were the accepted ways on every dairy farm.

There had to be a different way of working with animals!

I began to research other ways. I looked at animal charities and organisations and started to think about human behaviour with animals and indeed animal behaviour with humans.

My reading also led me toward animal psychology and that seemed to be the thing that excited me most. I started to read as many books as I could find on animal psychology particularly those by Konrad Lorenz and I became convinced that psychology and animal behaviour were the areas in which I wanted to work.

I found there was a course at Swansea University in psychology that had a lot of components of animal psychology, animal learning and animal behaviour.

I knew this was the one for me but would my 2'A' Level grades be enough to get me there?

What do I have to do to make it happen?

Chapter Four
Swansea and a Rat called Tess

Animal Behaviour, Animal Learning, Animal Psychology I knew immediately that was what I wanted to do.

I was now back in Aylesbury with my family and my next task was to somehow get a place at Swansea University. The literature from the UCAS [University Admission Service] made me doubt that my 'A' Level results were good enough. I was desperate to get onto the course at Swansea University but wasn't sure where to go from here. Dad was friendly with the Headmaster of the Grammar School and asked his advice.

'Tell Claire to send her cv to the head of the department she wishes to join at the University and include a letter of precisely why she wants to join Swansea University and take that particular course, I will make a call and tell him it is coming'.

I would obviously take his advice but thought – *'surely you can't get into University like that. What about UCAS? Don't they have to check and clear all applications before they even get submitted to a University? What happens if they turn me down?'*

'Claire just do as I suggest and you might be surprised.'

I was! I did as he suggested and within a week the Head of Department at Swansea University phoned me. I went to see him and I got accepted onto their BSc Psychology Course. I was beside myself with delight.

It was a campus university that fronted Swansea Bay. You could walk out of the campus straight onto the sands that were washed by the waters of the Atlantic at the start of the Bristol Channel. You could walk the sands right up to Mumbles Head if you wished. It was an idyllic place to study.

We were rapidly into Freshers' week where the hall was full of new students. It was a chance to meet up with other newcomers and be attracted to all the clubs that were available.

I signed up for horses, athletics, rugby, and the catholic society. I looked around. This was the next step in my life and I felt terrific awe and excitement.

At Swansea University you had to do three subjects in your Part One in the First Year. I opted for geography, philosophy, and psychology.

Psychology is split into different aspects – social psychology, animal learning & behaviour, ergonomics, and statistics. I loved the Animal Learning and Behaviour whereas a lot of people found it quite daunting.

This chapter starts with an illustration of one of the hamsters I trained at Swansea but quite soon into the course we were given a Rat.

Our task was to observe and train our rat to respond to our instructions. There were to be no negatives in our training – no giving electric shocks or inserting anything in the rat. You had to utilise and devise a system of rewards and instructions that the rat could follow and carry out.

Mine was a white rat with a black head and I immediately named it Tess after 'Tess of the D'Urbervilles' a book that I loved by Thomas Hardy set in my beloved Dorset.

The rat was to be with you at all times. You took your rat home in the holidays to continue your observations and training.

Introducing a live rat to my Mum and Dad was not without its humorous moments and I had to promise that Tess would not be allowed to run freely around the house and trash everything she could get her teeth into.

In fact Tess came to regard me as a trustworthy friend and would happily perch on me when I studied. I rapidly began to realise that you could communicate with a rat and if you observed it carefully enough you soon learned how a rat communicated to you.

I taught this rat to do everything you could think of. I learned the effects on the rat's behaviour of the timing of a reward, and what would happen if you changed that timing. I found that communicating with a rat was hugely stimulating to the rat and to me. I learned so much about animal behaviour from my lectures and from Tess that I decided it was time I got myself a dog,

Off I went to the rescue centre in Swansea but they wouldn't even consider me. I was a student living in a rented house with a number of other students and they made it clear that I had no chance of rescuing a dog. I got absolutely no-where with them. In a mood of huge disappointment I left the rescue centre.

As I was going out the gate I bumped into a family coming in. They were taking their dog to the centre. It appeared they were both working all day and the dog was shut up and had begun wrecking their home. They had given up on it. I couldn't stop myself –

'I'm looking for a dog, and I really wanted a spaniel please let me take him.'

'No, he is a real handful; I don't think you will be able to handle him'

'Oh I'm sure I can, look he's come to me straight away.'

I said this quickly as the dog lurched toward me almost pulling its owner off his feet.

'He's not really a bad dog,' said the owner, *'It's just that he is on his own all day while we are both out at work.'*

I was determined - *'Don't worry he will live with me and have plenty of company. I am a psychologist specialising in animal behaviour at the University. I am sure I can help him and give him a good home.'*

After many looks between the pair of them; Ruffles entered my life

Ruffles was a liver and white Spaniel, and had never been

trained. He was nearly uncontrollable!

He would leap on furniture, onto tables scattering everything in all directions. He wouldn't go on the lead, he was a complete handful.

If Claire Guest was ever to become a dog trainer here was a supreme challenge to start her on her way!

Everything I had done with the rat I tried on Ruffles and found it all worked really well. The timings of rewards, the amount, and the frequency all came into play. If I wanted to try something new I would try it on Tess first and then pick the best bits out and try it on Ruffles. Their reactions were almost identical.

Ruffles began to respond so well that within a year we were entering and winning obedience competitions. He was so good that I was allowed to take him into the university at certain times.

Swansea University was undertaking some of the earliest studies of the effects of taking dogs into homes for elderly people. They were monitoring the resident's blood pressures, heart rates etc.

and their responses whilst in the presence of a dog; also when stroking it and so on

My tutor was investigating of the effect of mutual grooming and was looking for a connection between stroking a dog and the instinctive reactions and pleasure that humans and other animals can get from mutual grooming.

Were the feelings you get from the grooming of your hair at the hairdressers similar to the feelings you and a dog get when you are stroking it? I was fascinated by all of this and Ruffles was used in many of the studies.

Despite my huge interest in the potential benefits of the relationship between dogs and people I actually chose the effects of oestrogen on behaviour of animals in my third year. I wanted to research how different foods might affect animal behaviour. I did a study looking at mice – comforted by the fact that Swansea University had very strict regulations about the welfare of animals.

I had groups of mice being fed different diets. Mice have a similar social structure to dogs. They live in groups. They relate and communicate to each other. Put one mouse in a box with another when they don't know each other then they will do things like a grooming, or diversion behaviour saying *'Hey I'm here don't hurt me'*, or they will go up to each other and say *'hello'*, or rapid tail thumping is warning the other *'don't get too close'*. I would observe them to see if different diets made them more hostile or less inclined to social behaviour or if it would change the way they responded to each other.

I had these groups of mice for a couple of months and I had to watch and video the mice behaviour night after night. If you can read mice behaviour then dog behaviour is much easier to understand. Mice behaviour is more subtle in the way they use the angle of their heads and their use of their eyes.

I came to love mice, they are very sweet animals.

I had hours and hours of mice behaviour on video and in the final study I was unaware of which group I was watching.

At that time I was also very interested in the behaviour of hamsters. I observed hamsters for hours on end but their behaviour was the very opposite to mice. Hamsters were very clean animals but have poor communication skills and little or no social behaviour. Put two hamsters who didn't know each other in the same box and they would try to kill each other.

My hours of observation and research did indicate that mice on a high soya diet were more aggressive and did engage in less social behaviour than mice on a normal food base.

Soya and wheatgerm both had high phytoestrogen (naturally occurring oestrogen) content. Since then studies on humans have indicated that high soya and oestrogen intake can also have an effect on behaviour.

So during my third year at Swansea University I had become obsessively interested in my mice. What they did, how they behaved. I would always have at least one mouse on me or in my pocket even when I went to church. I loved the feel of them on me and the way they curled their tails around my fingers. They were incredibly clean.

I had them on me all the time except when Mum made me promise I wouldn't bring my rat or my mice into the house on my visits home. I used to sneak the mice cages into the small cupboard under the eaves of the house. Mum never knew there could be mice in their cages under the eaves for the whole of the summer holidays.

Another study that I was subsequently to pursue was based around the 'Theory of Mind'. This covers the test of whether an animal has an understanding of how it relates to things around it and its place in the world rather than just exist. For many years it was thought that only humans were cognisant of their place in the world and that all animals were solely concerned with just existing.

Our training was though the Skinner Box. Its concept is that you can discover what an animal can learn without any human influence. You stay outside the Skinner Box which has a series of switches and lights. If the rat in the box pushes a switch it gets nothing, if it pushes another it gets a treat if it pushes another it gets three treats and so on. You have no influence so you observe how the rat behaviour is influence by its understanding of the consequence of events.

Simply put to show Theory of Mind the animal needs to be confronted with a problem, it must work out how it is going to solve that problem and then go solve it without using trial and error. If it tries it out without immediately solving the problem then Skinner calls it behaviourism, that the actions were conditioned by the results of behaviour rather than the mind working out a solution.

Years later I was to observe this behaviour with three of my dogs. Minstrel was a big powerful dog and if he had a bone there is no way the other two dogs could get it off him so they each tried a different technique. The female decided that outrageous flirtation was the way to get him to drop the bone so she could then grab it as her own. She would flutter her eyelashes at him make all the bitch on heat flirtation movements at him and try to tempt him to attractions of the flesh. Macho Minstrel would be tempted and she would get the bone.

When Ruffles had a bone it was much the same except that his temperament was different and she knew that he would not be at all interested in her flirtations. However she knew that if she went up to the front door and barked he would rush to the front door to see off or greet the visitor whilst she would double back and get the bone.

Skinnerism might claim that she learned through trial and error and thus this was behaviourism whereas it could be argued that no – she had worked out the different temperaments of the two dogs before she embarked upon the behaviour that would get her the bone and thus proved Theory of Mind.

I loved university life and though I was not back to the sheer happiness of my childhood in Dorset I did feel that I was beginning to find myself again.

From the time the lectures and tutorials started I loved everything about psychology particularly Animal Psychology.

From the very start I knew this is where my life belonged. It was a very good course and the lecturers pushed us to the limit but it all felt so right for me that I was totally comfortable. I found everything about the course to be fascinating, absolutely fascinating.

I would come back to Aylesbury in holidays and work try to earn a few pounds as a waitress at the Harrow Pub in Bishopstone. The diners were generous with their tips and the money made a big difference to what I was able to do when I returned to Swansea

The locals at the pub started to call me Freud as I would practice the psychology I had been taught on them. I started to read human behaviour so well that I would have a go at telling people's personality. Often locals would say to someone who was discussing as problem, *'Go see Freud; she'll soon sort you out'*

The person with the problem would come over to me and I would explain that it was only a hobby but they would say - *'Go on, tell me about myself, I want to know, tell me about myself'.*

I would tell them what their body language and personality was telling me and the inevitable repose was-

'How did you know that? Tell me more'.

I could inevitably tell them more because you could see it. The way they sat, the way they talked, the way they interacted with other people – it was all there for anyone to see if only they knew what to look for!

From our customer's continual requests I began to realise the insecurity that most people felt about their own world. They were struggling to come to terms with all that was happening around them. I could see that someone telling them

that they were actually like this or that was quite reassuring to them.

I was never 100% sure if my confidence in telling them their personalities came from an instinctive feeling I had from watching them or if it was a direct result of the lectures and course readings I had been absorbing.

In my second year at university I got called in by my Head of the Department. '

Claire, I assume you know you have a problem. Tests have revealed that you have a very poor capacity for facial recognition. Shown a picture of a face from one angle you are incapable of picking it out from another angle. A change of hair or growth of a moustache and you would have no idea who it was.'

I knew I had a problem as I used to remember people from their shoes, but didn't everybody do the same? It was only a problem when people changed their shoes. I then wouldn't know who they were unless they had some very strong facial features.

Whether this caused me to have to use some other method of recognition and communication they still did not know, nor had they identified how a different method would work.

It appears that I did not have this problem with animals but I seem to instantly know which animal it is and what it is feeling and thinking.

With dogs I get an instant communication even if I am driving past in a car. In the instant I have seen a dog walking along with or without its owners I know what the dog is thinking and what its lifestyle is.

From my infancy whenever I walked past an animal I got a sense of how they felt so I loved the opportunity the University gave for me to learn to communicate with all kinds of animals.

At that time in my life I used to think I also had good understanding and communications skills with people but an unmitigated disaster a few years later caused me to question that belief. With animals there was never a problem.

It is believed that animals with few exceptions do not have the cognoscente to deceive you. One of the exceptions might be the dog. The dog knows that if your back is to them and you are not watching they can take actions that can gain it a reward. Here again we are looking at the 'Theory of Mind'. The dog's behaviour would indicate that it had worked out its method of obtaining a reward rather that by acting through behaviourism and learning by trial and error.

'You are looking over there so I can steal this chocolate over here!'
Research is still investigation if a dog understands deception.

However they will give you unremitting love if you allow them. They are wonderful companions and I was receiving this every weekend as I was walked the sands of Swansea Bay with Ruffles.

From my involvement it can be seen that I enjoyed all parts of the course including human psychology. The bit that did not interest me highly was social psychology.

I had made a pal called Helen who was strongly into social psychology. She was a hoot and was extremely keen on absorbing all she could of that fascinating course of study.

Part of social psychology dealt with human 'deviant' behaviour including sexual deviations. At that time and unconnected to our course a number of female students rushed back into the college at various times visibly upset at having been 'flashed' at when walking on the sands of the bay.

The situation at Swansea was heaven sent for the 'flasher' – lots of female students walking the sands in pairs or on their own. The deviant would expose himself and get a thrill from the shocked reaction of the female student who usually rushed back into the safety of the campus.

Helen decided this presented a marvellous opportunity for her research into human sexual deviation and started walking the sands alone. After several days she was confronted by a 'flasher' exposing himself.

'Ah!' she said *'please don't move, please stay where you are, I'd like to talk to you'*

The 'flasher' was taken aback and didn't know how to handle the situation.

'I can help you, no don't go, I understand why you are doing this, please talk to me'

By now the 'flasher, was backing away aghast at the turn of events.

'Don't go, I can help you get over your problem'

Helen advanced toward him but in a mad panic he suddenly turned on his heel and rushed away. Helen ran after him all along the beach shouting *'Don't be afraid, I can help you.'*

She couldn't catch him and he rushed away ahead of her looking as if he was fleeing for his life with this attractive young lady rushing after him shouting *'Please stop, don't go, I understand why you are doing this, I can help you!'*.

All the students on the sands creased up laughing. Helen never got to research his problem as he was never seen on the sands again.

My life became walking on the beach at every opportunity with my lovely dog Ruffles, and observing and trying to influence the behaviour of various animals.

I had lived in hall of residents in my first year but got myself a little flat further along the beach for the rest of my time in Swansea.

I got a horse to ride and would often ride with the wife of the Principal of one part of the University. Mine was a young horse and was difficult to prepare – being very highly strung.

Roger Mugford was at that time perhaps U.K's leading expert in dog training and obedience. He came along to the University and gave us a lecture on animal behaviour. He was brilliant and I knew that was exactly what I wanted to do. I wrote to him and he kindly suggested I visit him spend a few days working with some dogs he was training. He was incredibly kind to me.

He had just developed the flexi lead.

These leads are well known now but I had never seen one before and had no idea how to use it. The lead runs out from a reel in the handlers hand so the dog is still on a lead even when 30 feet or more away. There is a small trigger on the reel that the handler loosens to let the dog go out 30 or so feet away or can reel the dog back and walk the animal on a normal length lead.

There was a dog on the lead when it was handed to me and it immediately shot the full 30 feet away. I had no idea that I could reel the dog back in to me and it rushed about in all directions before going round and round a tree and me so I was helpless lassoed to the tree and had to be rescued.

Roger had seen all this and quite kindly said *'Claire, you're a lovely person but you should think of another career. Dog trainer is probably not the right career for you'*

I couldn't believe it! The foremost dog trainer in England had just told me that I wasn't cut out to be a dog trainer. I returned to university absolutely gutted!

My whole world had been turned upside down.

This man had decided that dog training was not the right career for me but that was all I wanted to do.

On my return to the college I discovered that there was a big party at the university. I remember getting incredibly drunk on some stuff someone had brought back from Greece. I was told that I spent the entire party muttering in a drunken rage.

'Roger Mugford says I'll never be a dog trainer. What does he know; I'll show him how to be a dog trainer. I'll show him, I'll show him, that Roger Mugford. I'm going to be the best dog trainer in the world'

I don't remember getting to bed.

Unfortunately I was due out riding with the Principal's wife the next morning and she was a really early bird.

My alarm went off and I had to go out but I was still nearly paralytic from the previous night's party. The room was spinning, my head was going round and round – how I managed to get dressed I'll never know. I couldn't stop my stagger as I walked to the horses. When tacking up I fell against the horse in a drunken stupor but somehow managed to get his tack on him and then climbed aboard scarcely able to sit steadily.

The principal's wife used to go galloping off all over the place and having asked me if I was alright off we set with me just clinging onto my mount for all I was worth. How I didn't fall off and kill myself I never did know. It must have been all the practice I had in my early years riding in Dorset.

Sober the next day I cycled down to the university with the bike laden with the multitude of psychology journals I needed to read.

I regularly cycled to and from university along by the seafront and sometimes the wind was so strong it would almost blow me backwards. The huge pack of books and journals in a pack on my back would catch the wind and I would often be pedalling getting nowhere. But I loved this time. I had lots of friends and every minute was interesting. I didn't find it hard work.

When lecturers explained theory many students were screwing their faces up as they tried to get to grips with it but I seemed to instantly understand the subject and the theory. It didn't need any further explanation.

It was like – *'I get that, yep I get that, and that, and that!'* it was all so clear. I just knew this was for me.

I loved the course work, the lectures, tutorials and all the research but the exams for a Batchelor of Science Degree (BSc) at the end of my third year caused me a lot of anxiety. It meant so much to me. My course work had hovered around the First/2.1 level but my 'A' Level results at Aylesbury High had been a big disappointment and I did not want that to happen again. I had to hope that the knowledge I had acquired from 3 years of hard work, only slightly diminished by the accompanying three years of hard play, was sufficient to gain the qualification I so wanted.

I have to admit to discoing, partying, riding, walking the sands, and having a wonderful and active social life at the same time as working very hard on my studies.

I was awarded an Upper 2.1.

A 2.1 pass was fantastic but I would have loved to have achieved a First. I was told that I only marginally missed it.

So I became Claire Guest BSc (Hons).

The Honours came from the research I had completed in my three years at University.

Maybe if I had done nothing other than study I might have got a First but the active social life I had enjoyed undoubtedly made me a more rounded person and better able to cope with life.

When out at the many parties and discos I would have a drink but never to excess after my reaction to Roger Mugford's comments. It was the music and dancing I enjoyed the most and couldn't get enough of. I didn't know then that music was to become very important to me later in my life.

I thought I would stay on at Swansea hoping to apply for a Master's Degree, but instead decided to spend the summer looking after a small holding that belonged to the lady whose flat I had rented.

In my time at Swansea I had lived on Campus first year and then rented flats in Mumbles and again in the Uplands. Some of the flats were in awful condition and would have been condemned in today's world; mind you they were occupied by combinations of University Students

I eventually stayed in my Dad's caravan that he had towed to Swansea and was based at Three Cliffs Bay.

I needed very little to live on. Charity shops were a source for my clothing and I was always quite careful with my money. Mum and Dad provided me with funds if I was in real need but I used to work in pubs and help out at a local vet's practice so managed to survive and pay my way on very little.

The vet was a real 'Uncle Herriot' with a wicked sense of humour. In my first year at Swansea I was training a couple of hamsters to do all sorts of things. I always had a hamster about my person and loved them to bits. Hamsters are very clean animals, you could put it into its cage to go to the toilet and it would and then get back onto you and stay perfectly clean until you next put it back in its cage.

My hamster called Asher became very ill. I had no money but I knew I had to get her to a Vet. I looked in Yellow Pages and found a vet to whom I could walk up to in the Uplands and that's how I met Julian Hudson who ran a small veterinary practice with his wife.

I immediately realised that he was doing his best to save my hamster Asher but we discovered she had stripped the paint on the bars of the cage I had kept her in and she could not recover from digesting the chemicals in the paint or the metal.

It is always heart-breaking to lose an animal and Julian Hudson had been most kind. I told him what I wanted to do in life he told me that he had just come to Swansea to set up his own practice and he couldn't pay me but I was welcome to help out if it suited me. He promised that he would teach me all he could and he was true to his word.

He always treated my pets and animals free of charge so I was gaining a great practical education into life as a Vet and the stress of paying veterinary bills for all my animals was removed.

I worked with him as often as I could throughout my time in Swansea although in my third year I had moved down into Mumbles and then extra studies as my finals approached cut down the time I had available.

I learnt a terrific amount about animal welfare from Julian and kindness to the animals and their owners. He allowed me in when he was operating on animals and talked me through everything he was doing. It gave me a huge understanding of the physiology of animals that was to be a great help to me as I progressed my studies.

I often sat and comforted the owners when their animals were being put down and here I really began to understand the huge bond there was between the animals and their owners and the huge love they had for each other.

After my finals I spent a lot of time on the beach reading every book on animal behaviour I could get my hands on. I would read books on dog training whether I felt the content was good or bad. I was quite critical of some books and didn't agree with their methods as the best way to train a dog or any animal.

My work at the vets convinced me that there must be a better way of training animals and in particular dogs than many of the ways recommended by 'experts'. I had witnessed in the three years the grief of owners whose dogs were at the end of their lives and knew the huge love they had for their dogs, and the dogs had for them. They deserved a far better method of working and living together than the crude methods of discipline that were often used and even more often recommended in books on training animals.

I was aware of the deep relationship that animals – particularly dogs have with humans and if they were to live together there must be a way of ensuring that both the human and the dog gets the best out of it.

I knew it must be wrong to force unnatural behaviour onto a dog. Rubbing a puppy's nose in any mistake it had made had to be wrong. You don't act that way with a human baby! Forcing the dog to act only as the human wants, dominating and smacking a dog with newspapers, wrenching on check leads, why should all this be right when the dog loves its human and its owner loves their dog. There has to be a better way!

Many of these books were really advocating that you must dominate this animal - sometimes quite savagely. I knew that this could not be right.

People in my department at Swansea were researching the effects that dogs were having on people just being in contact with them. It seemed to have beneficial effects on heart rate, blood pressure, tranquillity and a whole range of psychological benefits. I was very privileged to be part of that research.

As it was my studies had taken me to a BSc(Hons) so at the end of the summer came decision time.

Do I go on with studies and try for a Masters Degree; or perhaps even a PhD; or go back to Aylesbury and the family I deeply loved get a 'proper job'; and consider my future and maybe decide on what I really could achieve in life.

Dave from Home Farm in Devon had come up to Swansea quite a lot over the three years. In my second year he decided he would leave the farm and move up with me on a permanent basis. As eldest child and therefore the designated inheritor of the farm this was a big, big decision. He found work locally in Swansea as a landscape gardener. He was now willing to move with me up to Aylesbury and stop in separate rooms with my Mum and Dad.

- Do I follow my dream wherever it should take me?
- Do I take a 'proper job' and do something sensible?
- Do I find a house of my own and share it with Dave.
- Do I get married, which would mean a full Catholic ceremony at St Joseph's?
- Do I settle down and raise a family?
- Am I willing to sacrifice any further chance of study and University?

Time to go home to Aylesbury and consider all the options.

When back home the influences all around me were to take the option of taking a 'proper job', settle down, and get married!

For a short while this almost worked.

Claire Guest
"Listened to Daisy"

Chapter Five
'A Proper Job'

Twenty-three years old and a 'proper job' at last!

I had got a good job, 9–5 flexi-hours, £8,750 a year with an index linked civil service pension, good holidays.

What more could I wish for?

I could afford to pay my own way in life, have a little car, and even buy a house.

Assistant Scientific Officer in the Timber Preservation Department at the Building Research Establishment in Princes Risborough, Buckinghamshire might seem an unlikely place to find Claire Guest at the end of her time in Swansea. I had really planned to do a Masters Degree but I wanted a Masters by Research and I had missed the deadline for applying for a bursary.

Mum and Dad and the bit I could earn waitressing in the pubs had paid my way to date but I was now 23 years old and my parents had three other girls to finance through their education. The 'Masters' was therefore not an option – certainly not at that time.

If I were to get a bursary then Mum and Dad said that they would help financially if we could work out a way of paying my way through the research. However it certainly was not possible for at least for a year so perhaps it was better to give up such thoughts.

Scientific Assistant was to be my full time job and my future.

Dave and I had been sleeping in separate rooms at Mum and Dad's so the next logical decision was for us to find a place of our own.

We purchased a cottage in Steeple Claydon, a few miles north-west of Aylesbury and in our day living together in a place of our own meant marriage.

Dave had left the farm during my second year at Swansea and had lived with me in the various flats we shared with other students. He had come back up to Aylesbury with me and was happy with landscape gardening as his future.

He was an incredibly sincere man and I had no doubts about marrying him. We had known each other for a long time and life was about doing the right thing so it was to be marriage and a mortgage.

Ruffles my dog was still with me and I still had some mice and hamsters but the rat Tess had been found new a home. When the degree course had ended at Swansea the rat, hamsters and mice were due to go back to the university where they would be gassed to death. They couldn't be used for further research as they had already been through a course of training with me. The alternative to the death sentence was for me to find a new home for them.

'You wouldn't fancy re-homing a nice little mouse would you?'

This was my common question every time I met anybody and everybody. When they backed away I would produce this lovely looking mouse from somewhere on my person and hold it so that it could look so appealingly at them.

'Please give it a home otherwise it will be killed. Look it's beautiful but will be gassed if I cannot find a home for it. It is fully trained and will be a great companion for you. You will love him.'

Enough of my friends and acquaintances were kind enough to home one or more of my mice and gradually I got them all rehomed. Tess was adopted by another friend as a pet rat but not before I had let it out for a run one time when at my mother's house. I couldn't find her for days I knew mother would go spare if she knew that there was a rat loose somewhere in her house. Thankfully Tess turned up before Mum knew I had sneaked her into our home. It was pleasing that Tess lived a happy life with a friend from University and eventually died of old age.

I had 40 mice in my research groups so by the time I had finished finding a new home for them I knew all my friends had a lovely pet white mouse, or two, or more.

With most of my mice and rats re-homed it was onto the Timber Preservation Department at the Building Research Establishment in Princes Risborough and to life in the lovely village of Steeple Claydon in Bucks.

I was an Assistant Scientific Officer researching timbers and how long they survive when in contact with the soil, with or without various forms of timber treatment, and how they were affected by different levels of moisture.

In the middle of Thetford Forest in Norfolk there lots of wooden stakes that have been driven into the ground. The stakes are made up from different woods imported from all over the world. Once a year the Assistant Scientific Officer would accompany a Scientific Officer into the Forest and bang a series of these stakes to see if they break.

The Scientific Officer I worked with was very kind and had a great sense of humour so visits to Thetford Forest banging stakes and bringing the broken bits back to Princes Risborough for chopping up and analysis became very enjoyable. We would research the chopped up wood to determine the effects of different levels of pressure used when injecting preservatives into the timber and the job became a most enjoyable and stress fee way of earning a living.

The results of our research were sent out to Building Controllers and Regulators who could advise the trade and check that wood used in houses and other buildings had been properly treated.

I actually enjoyed this work far more that I was expecting. It was a very easy going department and I was very comfortable here. It would have been very easy to make it a lifetime's career but I somehow always had a feeling that it probably would not fill a lifetime's role for me.

When I was working from the office I would go for a run with Ruffles most lunchtimes on a circular route of footpaths that went up into the surrounding hills and onto Bledlow Ridge and then back down through the Public Footpaths to Princes Risborough.

One day I paused and stood at the top of the Ridge and looked across the hills and fields.

That day they had a different light illuminating them and an event occurred that has happened to me a number of times in life. A feeling enveloped me. Sometimes these feelings are reassuring and sometimes they are very worrying. On this occasion the light across the valley seemed different and I immediately felt that there was going to be a change. I somehow knew that there would be dramatic changes in my life.

I had a mixture of excitement and concern that such events always caused me.

Within a few days an advert in the local newspapers leapt out at me. It was for a Dog Trainer at a charity called Hearing Dogs at Stokenchurch in the Chiltern Hills.

Hearing Dogs at that time consisted of just 3 people with ambitious plans. The job paid less than half the salary I was getting at the Building Research Department and had no pension or other perks. It would be madness to apply for it and yet it excited me.

I wasn't looking for another job. I was very content where I was. If I was going to change it was going to be back to Swansea University to research for my Masters Degree.

Yet I couldn't get this advert out of my mind. Somehow I knew that it was going to change my life.

Chapter Six
Hearing Dogs

I had seen the advertisement and applied, was met by Tony Blunt and taken into a bedroom that he was using as an office in the bungalow that was on the site. He sat me down and showed me the plans he had drawn up showing what the site was going to look like,

'These would be our kennels – this area will be for training, here will be our offices'.

I couldn't see how he would achieve any of this but he was absolutely passionate about it.

He asked me a few questions about my experience with dogs and my beliefs and we got on very well. He rang me next day at work and offered me the job and I accepted.

I think Mum and Dad thought I was mad to take the job at half my present salary, no pension or perks, but when I stressed that it was what I wanted to do they were fine with it.

The first dog I trained on my own was named Lisa and pronounced Leesa. Liza was the dog we'd had since my time at Aylesbury High School and was still alive and living with Mum and Dad in Aylesbury.

Hearing Dogs had only been going for about 3 years before I joined them and Tony had trained their first few dogs but then began to get bogged down in admin and getting the money in, so the training was handled by a trainer they had at that time.

My work with the rat and Ruffles enabled me to work out how all the bits of training fitted together. The principle of training the dogs was not vastly different to all the principles I used on Tess – my rat at Swansea University.

We were offering rewards to the dog based on its responses to situations you created during training - the ringing of a doorbell, of a phone, a door knocker and so on.

At first the dog must do thing 'number one' to get a reward,

and then learns that it must do thing 'number one and thing number two' to get the reward.

And then it must do thing 'numbers one, two and three' to get the reward and so on. (A method of training known as 'chaining').

The concept of all animal training is thus straightforward. As long as the trainer is absolutely consistent in their requirements the animal will respond if it wants the reward.

The thing that was very interesting for me was the concept of needing to train a dog that is going to perform perfectly even when it has been given to somebody else – in the case of hearing dogs it would be with the deaf person with whom the dog was to live for the rest of its life.

So it was no longer about me being able to control that dog or me being able to work with the dog but it was about - can I give that dog the knowledge it needs and can I then transfer that knowledge onto another person?

This whole area was completely new to me.

The dog was to be trained to respond to sounds and needed to respond correctly at least 90% of the time. In those days we trained the dogs to respond correctly to six sounds (nowadays we try for 8 or more). They were; -

Alarm Clock,
Door Bell,
Door Knocker,
Telephones specially adapted for deaf people,
Cooker timer,
and Smoke Alarm

We progressed them later to a sound that told them to go and fetch help. These were the 'core sounds'. Some dogs only managed four sounds but made good working dogs.

We had a dog for 16 weeks so we had to achieve successful response to six sounds in that time. This became a little easier once Hearing Dogs developed its own puppy-walking scheme but at the time I joined them nearly all the dogs came from Rescue Centres.

The dogs might therefore have strong independent characteristics but if they were chosen by us then within 16 weeks they must be capable of being placed with a hard-of-hearing person and respond successfully to 6 or more core sounds.

I really enjoyed going to the rescue centres and finding the dogs to train. In those days there was still a genuine problem with strays and so there were a whole variety of dogs in rescue centres. Nowadays the microchip has reunited many stray dogs with their owners and we have seen the trend towards specially bred dogs at rescue centres. Staffies (Staffordshire Bull Terriers) and other dogs often end up there when they became difficult due to their owners inability or lack of knowledge on how to handle them, or where the owner simply got bored.

There were some lovely dogs at rescue centres and in time they allowed me to be with a dog I managed to develop a way of reliably assessing its behaviour. My method was based on assessments that are made in human psychology that are being increasingly used in the assessment of animal behaviour.

In humans you can ask a series of carefully chosen questions that will reveal the tendency of person being questioned to pessimism or optimism and to introvert or extrovert behaviour. All normal human behaviour can be placed within these categories.

Careful observation of a dog will allow you to similarly analyse that animal under the same headings. This has enormous importance if you are trying to predict how a dog will react in a particular situation and is particularly relevant to assistance dogs. What you are trying to assess is not only how well will this dog take to the training but also what will it's temperament now be and how will it behave for the next 10 years.

It is possible to do some tests to see how the dog is reacting now but if you can get beneath that and find out what is the dog's core temperament is then you can make predictions about how that dog is going to behave over it's lifetime.

It is reasonably easy to see how extrovert (sociable) a dog is by the way it reacts when meeting new people or situations. If a dog is to become an assistance dog you can train an extrovert that is slightly neurotic because if it is sufficiently extrovert it will get over it's anxiety by watching other dogs and other people and gaining confidence.

When confronted with new situations the neurotic will tend to cling to you but its extrovert characteristic will rapidly allow it to see that there is nothing to be frightened about and it will quickly re-learn behaviour and gain confidence.

Many Labradors fall into this category *'If the gang says its o.k. then I'll go along with it'*

However the neurotic that is slightly introverted will not want to get involved but will slink away saying *'I'm not doing that again'.*

Dogs are often bred to act in a fixed way. Fighting dogs and Guard dogs are typical examples. Staffordshire Bull Terriers (Staffies) and Pit Bull Terriers have sometimes been bred to attack and be fearful of nothing. They usually don't re-learn easily.

Assistance dogs need to be extrovert.

They have to go everywhere with their owners – into public places, on buses, trains, into public buildings, offices and work premises, and so on so they have to be confident and like people.

The dog needs to learn quickly and the neurotic learns much faster than the psychotic.

My studies in psychology at Swansea University resulted in the definition and analysis proving relatively straightforward for me but often puzzling for others.

I had developed these techniques whilst assessing dogs and they resulted in a great success rate (nearly twice the assessment success rate the charity achieved in later years). People were asking me to explain how I managed it and I tried to explain but most folk had problems understanding the characteristics that placed a person or dog into introvert; extrovert, psychotic; neurotic categories. They couldn't seem to see that you can relatively easily observe these traits in the dog's responses to events that surrounded it.

I was able to use so much of the information and techniques I had used in my studies at Swansea University to help in the selection and training of dogs at Hearing Dogs.

When selecting a dog from a rescue centre you usually had about 15 minutes to come up with an assessment but they would normally allow me to take the dog into reception and watch how it reacted to the comings and goings. I could take it out into the field and see how it responded, put it on a lead and walk it around the site – all of this would give you the clues to the dog's personality, behaviour and response to stress and it's recovery time.

If I wasn't certain I would ask the rescue centre if I could sit in reception with the dog for a while and observe how it reacted. So often a dog is fearful from having been lost or finding itself in such unfamiliar surroundings but they may not actually be as nervous as it appears but shell-shocked.

I would be more ready to take on such a dog than I would a dog that was clearly showing that it didn't want to know or embrace anything new.

Some of the other trainers who used this method of assessing and training a dog would get too involved in the detail. They would see a single action from the dog and allow it to colour their entire assessment. They would even re-assess its training needs without looking at the dog as a whole and taking in the need to look at the whole picture.

I began to get very high success rates for dogs that I had selected and during my time at Hearing Dogs I trained a whole host of lovely dogs.

Lisa belonged to a lovely lady from Scotland. She didn't really want to part with beloved Labrador for 16 weeks and I could understand why. Lisa was a lovely looker – almost pure white – and I promised the lady that if we had her I would take her home with me every night. She trained very well and acted as a Hearing Dog for her owner for the rest of her life.

I took many dogs home with me whilst I was training them. One with a huge personality was –

SOOTY

 - a little black mongrel made up of all bits and pieces so you couldn't tell what breeds he came from. He was about the size of a cocker spaniel and had been part of a litter that had been hit by Parvovirus.

He was so smart and it was an inspiration to see a dog like him. You would teach him to do something and he not only got it straight away but would be looking at you as if saying *'o.k. got that – so come on what else?*

He became the most fantastic Hearing Dog. He worked to eight sounds which at that time was unique. He went to a completely deaf lady and developed even more ways of helping her. He would do things like dragging his bed with him into each room the lady was then occupying so she always had his company and help should she need it.

He also gave me one of my messiest and smelliest catastrophes when I had him at home during his training period. I must have been tired and was asleep when he started to make a fuss. I ignored him and told him to go away – I needed to sleep. He kept creating a fuss and I asked him

'What on earth is wrong with you? Now go and lie down'

He did but when I got up in the night and walked down the stairs something squelched under my feet and between my toes. Poor Sooty had suffered chronic diarrhoea and the stairs and the landing were covered as were my feet. He had then walked it all over the house

'Sooty what have you done!' I exclaimed and I can still see his poor little face looking up at me with his expression and entire body language saying –

'I'm sorry, I'm sorry - I have been trying to tell you for the last half an hour that I needed to go out to be clean but I'm sorry!'

Silly me! I resolved to always listen to my dogs in future.

Sooty really was a lovely lovely dog.

Dogs have personalities of their own and many of those I have trained stand out in my memory. Some have touched my heart and will always be there.

WOODY

Woody was a handsome looking chocolate brown Cocker Spaniel that soon after birth developed some severe physical problems.

When I first saw him as a very young puppy he was crawling along dragging his back legs behind him. He couldn't stand or reach his mother's teats as she stood to feed her puppies.

It seemed there was no hope for him but as I walked into

the kennels he looked up at me in a way that made him irresistible.

From the look on his face you just had to think that this little puppy deserved a chance of normal or nearly normal life. He was going to be put down but I persuaded the breeder to let me have the pup and off went 'Woody' to a new home – ours!

Once home it was obvious that Woody had no control over his back legs and no hope of a normal life so having him put down had to be a serious option. We decided to get the vet's opinion but on the way there Woody licked my hands so lovingly and looking down into his liquid brown eyes I became convinced that we must do all we could for this little pup.

The vet's analysis confirmed that Woody suffered a paralysis in the back legs, cause unknown, but he was certain that the puppy was pain free so back home he went with us. With regular feeding he began to progress at home until the illness started to affect his back and his left eye began to close. The battle to give him a good life seemed lost.

Back to the vet's for what we expected to be the last time for Woody when the vet suddenly thought that Woody might be suffering from neospora – a parasite that is rare in dogs although they can be carriers but fairly common in cattle.

It was worth trying something different. Blood tests were taken and analysed by Liverpool University Hospital but Woody was deteriorating fast despite the treatment recommended by the vet.

It looked as though he was dying but the day following our 'last' visit to the vet I thought he looked a little brighter and three days later there was a noticeable wag of a tail.

Two weeks later Woody managed to get to his feet and his tail started to wag semi-vigorously, never to stop. He could stand but could not co-ordinate his back legs. One leg was paralysed completely. He would try to walk but would fall over and then drag his legs behind him. He suffered no pain but he would never regain the full use of his back legs.

People had begun to regard me as an outstanding dog trainer. Was I good enough to teach this lovely little dog how to overcome his disability and move around under his own volition? He was such a lovely dog but it was to be quite a challenge.

I would start Woody swimming – our bath was large enough as Woody was so small – follow with weeks of physiotherapy with many different exercises, all the while training him to respond to the clicker.

Clicker training for Woody was to teach him how to gain control of his back legs and take short steps. I also taught him how to turn without falling over. With the click there was a reward and soon he was having all kinds of fun by responding to the clicker.

Woody loved the improvement the clicker brought to him and thus loved the training. Gradually he learned to walk!

He began to embrace life to the full and went to the office every day with me. He did a

wonderful demonstration with me when I gave a talk on the marvels of clicker training to the Association of Pet Behaviour Counsellors (APBC).

He grew into a life of laughter, wagging and full of fun. The hair never grew on his bottom, or parts of his leg or tail but to the end of his life he skipped along as happy a dog as you could ever wish to see. He was my constant companion for the $14^1/_2$ he was with me. I had saved his life and he thanked me for this everyday, he helped me through what was to be my life's greatest challenge, always by my side with his infectious enthusiasm. The day Woody died I thought I would never recover, but now I remember his happiness, his strength of character and his complete devotion. I had been truly blessed.

Claire Guest
"Listened to Daisy"

I had achieved my Master of Science and in the years ahead would be awarded a Doctorate. Dr Claire Guest BSc (Hons) MSc – wow what an achievement - Mum and Dad were so proud.

Claire Guest
"Listened to Daisy"

People had started applying for dogs from Hearing Dogs to help them overcome some of the problems their deafness caused them.

The charity had got a lot bigger and I was by then responsible for the training whilst Gillian Lacey looked after the placing of the dogs and the training of their new owners.

Gill had told me years before about her dalmatian dog. The dog had persistently licked or sniffed at a mole and had been so focused on it that Gill had to keep pushing the dog away. Eventually Gill went to her G.P. and had the mole removed. She was called several days later to be told that the mole had been a malignant melanoma. The dog's behaviour had saved her life – the melanoma being cut out before it had become fatal.

Gill's story always stayed in my mind and along with similar anecdotal stories became the impetus many years later for me to investigate whether dogs really could 'sniff out' cancer and other life threatening diseases.

At that time all of the research into that subject was way in the future and my main concern was training dogs to be successful and efficient hearing dogs for the rest of their lives.

Gill would check out the applicants and come to me to see what dogs I had in training. We would then discuss what we felt was the best match between dog and owner.

The new owner would stay at the centre for a week (in the early days before we had accommodation for them they would stay at the local Bed and Breakfast). I would do the week at the centre matching the training of dog and owner then Gill would take responsibility for them and any home support that was necessary.

Most of the early applicants were women but I did train a dog for a gentleman who lived in Northern Ireland. It was the time of the Troubles and my trips to Northern Ireland were scary. My client lived on a road that had one of the biggest problems in the Troubles and I had been warned to look under my car every morning to make sure there was not a bomb there. Apparently my hire car with English car number plates could be enough for a fanatic to place a bomb under it.

One night I was staying at a lady's house after doing some fund-raising just outside Belfast and I was a bit nervous of the situation in Northern Ireland at that time.

I was a Catholic lady driving an English car – so who do I ask if I am in trouble? Do I seek out a Catholic helper or a Protestant?

I had driven into this little village and luckily found a nice house to stay at with a kindly lady. She provided an evening meal and off I went to bed. She had told me that we were close to the troubles but they occurred farther down the road. However in the middle of the night there was a massive explosion of noise.

It was the biggest noise I had ever heard. I lay in the bed checking myself out and was delighted to feel that I seemed to be completely intact and not damaged in the explosion.

I was in one piece so I got up and looked out of my bedroom window and could see smoke and dust billowing around. I went downstairs to see if the lady knew what had happened.

It turned out that a soldier had just come back from being billeted in Germany where they drive on the right side of the road. He set off late at night on the wrong side of an Irish road and had needed to swerve violently to avoid an oncoming vehicle, had lost control of his car and smashed into the corner of the house I was staying in. As I went downstairs I found a car in the room below my bedroom. The ceiling of the room was damaged but intact otherwise I would have found myself on top of the car and the debris in nothing but my pyjamas.

I had a number of scares on my trips but that was the one that shook me most.

Generally most applicants for Hearing Dogs had a love of dogs but the problems always arose when you feel that the owner doesn't. I had a very strong belief that you only get the full joy of a relationship between a dog and its owner if both parties want it and give to that relationship.

It is always a mistake placing a dog with a person who does not appreciate that it is a living thing with a character and a soul. Some owners treat the dog a bit like a machine thinking it will react to everything as though they just need to push a button and it will do what they want. Most dogs want to please, they will try hard to succeed, to read what we want and adapt their behaviour readily to seek our approval. This wish is enhanced by a strong relationship.

Once you have severely scolded or worst still hit a dog then that love relationship by which the dog will do all it can to help and love you takes a lot of repairing and many times cannot be re-established.

I am sad to admit that I've had dogs in the past that after a really tough time at work or in my personal life I've shouted at even though I have known that the dog has not really understood what I wanted. I have always regretted it. It has really spoiled the relationship I had enjoyed with that dog.

Once you have broken that trust between you and a dog you never completely rebuild it. You might come close and manage to build a working relationship but that deep trust will be gone and will never come back.

I'd like to think I learned from those occasions and would now stop my emotional response; take a step back and reconsider the situation so that I can help the dog to understand what I want without confusing it further with my outburst.

When you first start down any career path or set of actions it is very easy for the human ego to start to intrude.

You want to be seen to be the best sportsman in your group or the best manager in your firm or the best dog trainer in your charity and this can shorten the temper and create frustrations when anything intrudes on that goal. It is not always easy to put the ego on one side and concentrate on the object of your exercise as your main priority; - the needs of the team, the welfare and success of your company and fellow workers; the needs of the individual dog.

Appreciating the need of the ego and the ability to put it to one side when necessary seems to be one of the hardest lessons to learn in life but perhaps one of the most vital. If you can retain your determination to succeed but take the ego out of the step you are about to take in life then surprisingly it takes all the worry away and hugely increases your chance of success.

I was enjoying success at Hearing Dogs but I had to learn to lose my ego!

Over the 20 years I was with them I had progressed from Trainer to Head Trainer to Training Manager to Director of Training to Director of Operations. I had 70 staff responsible for up to 60 dogs under training at any one time and the organisation had grown to 146 staff in two main locations.

I should have been deliriously happy but I wasn't!

I was also growing increasingly unhappy by my seeming inability to get the Trainers at Hearing Dogs to train in the manner and to the standards I needed. I was beginning to feel hugely frustrated at my position and life had become really miserable.

The demands of my work as Director of Training resulted in me being remote from the dogs. I would tend to be called in to see 'difficult' dogs and this would increase my frustration.

I decided that I needed to start up something that would get me back in direct contact with dogs once more.

I prepared and submitted my portfolio and became a registered canine behaviourist. I was then able to go and advise people who were having behaviour difficulties with their dogs.

I become a member of the Association of Pet Behaviour Counsellors (APBC - the governing body for animal behaviourists in the U.K) and later became Chair.

I was amazed to find myself Chairman of the leading body for animal behaviour in the U.K. whilst still working at Hearing Dogs. After 6 years in the post my deteriorating domestic situation led me to resign the chair of the A.P.B.C. but I was then elected as the first honorary lifetime member.

My behaviour work was a hobby. I also got involved in developing and training gun dogs. I was horrified at the way many owners treated their gun dogs and knew there must be a better way.

Many gun dog trainers were beating up their dogs in an effort to train them. Some used electric collars, many regularly kicked and otherwise ill-treated their dogs so I decided that I would train my own gun dogs and see if we could get top rate performance without brutalising their training.

By now my frustrations with my job at Hearing Dogs and in my personal life with a husband who worked with me were causing me to hate each day I spent in the office. A change of Chief Executive at Hearing Dogs had brought a change of style of management from absolute trust to constant questioning and this heaped even more frustration onto my life. My time with the gun dogs and those with behavioural problems was a blessing for it was keeping me sane.

When out with the gun dogs it was just me and the dogs in the woods training to retrieve and present the retrieve to my hand. I trained my own dogs and wanted to see if I could train them up to the highest level without resorting to the brutal methods used by others. I got them to the highest level and my dogs were competing against the top gun dogs in the U.K.

I remember standing on a beautiful heather clad Scottish hillside in competition with the country's top gun dog trainer. He had won the National Field Trial Championships many times and for the previous three years.

'Claire, when your dogs are working why do you keep clicking that clicker you have in your hand?'

'This clicker tells the dog I am training that that he has just done exactly what I want. When he hears the click he knows that there is a reward for him. He knows that the quartering pattern he has just performed was exactly right and the click tells him that he has earned a reward.'

His reaction was very interesting –

'You know how dogs are trained up here? They know they've done right because they haven't had a bollicking!'

That taught me something! The method of training he described can be very successful and many dogs trained that way were champions. It took my mind back to Swansea University and training my rat Tess.

There were the two ways of training a rat and in the sense of performance the results are not that much different. In the sense of the animal's welfare the methods were poles apart.

These periods when I was out with the dogs were exciting and I dreaded having to return to my office. This made me hugely frustrated because I had always wanted to work with dogs and here was I responsible for the training of 60 dogs at any one time. It helped me to get over my frustrations to think of the difference that the dogs would make to their owners. The trained dog could dramatically improve their lifestyle.

What could be a better way of working for a living?

So why wasn't I happy?

Indeed why was I so unhappy?

***

Chapter Seven
Soul Mates Traumas

We had a young man apply to Hearing Dogs for a job. He had just finished his degree in Modern Languages at Trinity College Cambridge and had run a dog club at University. He wanted to get involved at Hearing Dogs. He asked if he could start in the kennels. I was still a Trainer in those early days and Tony Blunt – the boss who had employed me asked me to interview him and report back what I thought.

He was in his early twenties, blond, angelic face, high rosy cheeks, and a fine physique. It was all I could do to concentrate on the questions I had prepared for the interview. His responses were outstanding. He was so much in sync with our plans and goals that his whole outlook reminded me of me, he could have been my twin brother - a soul-mate in the making. He got the job!

He really was beautiful and seemed to be everything a girl would want and he made it clear he felt the same way about me. I fell head over heels in love with him leading to divorce from Dave and marriage to my 'soul mate'

Early in our marriage a few shocking events should have warned me of the traumas to come but I ignored them – hopelessly in love! We settled down to a blissful living - training dogs and competing with them and our horses.

Fifteen years on and a number of challenging events culminating in our competition for the top post at work created a great deal of tension between us and unfortunately our marriage started to unravel. The bliss was replaced by tension, stress and led to scenes only experienced in nightmares.

Our marriage ended in events so traumatic I had a complete nervous and emotional breakdown that took every ounce of strength I had to bring about a recovery. I find I am unable to discuss or write about the shock and traumas I suffered and feel we must pass over those awful events and move on with life.

Chapter Eight
The Blissful Years

I had wanted to join the APBC and that was a lot of hard work getting a portfolio together. When that was done I began to follow my love of gun dogs. I had two dogs at the time – Ruffles and Minstrel.

I was young and thought I could change the world of gundog ownership. I wanted to show gundog owners that you could train a dog to be outstanding without resorting to all the violence and unnecessary cruelty we had seen used by so many owners.

I thought we could train dogs through only positive methods without bullying and whenever I had spare time I would be training our dogs. Life was training dogs during the week and then going off to competitions with our own dogs at week-ends.

We qualified for National gundog Finals even though we were both very young to be competing at that level. We felt we were making some headway in changing perceptions on training methods when people would start to notice how well trained our dogs were and started to ask us about our methods.

Training and competing with our dogs was becoming a passion.

As a child I used to watch the *'Magic Roundabout'* on TV and loved the dog 'Dill'. It used to make me laugh and I can still repeat its sayings today. I always said that I wanted a working spaniel called Dill!

Working bred Cocker Spaniels weren't that popular at that time so I started looking for a dog that I could call Dill. One day at a field trial a gentleman said to me that he had a litter of puppies at home and they were cocker spaniels. Off I went to see them and one had this lovely big face that looked out at me with such trust. He looked me straight in the eye with such an enquiring look I thought *'That's Dill'* and so this puppy went home with me and became Dill.

He turned out to be the most fantastic dog you could imagine. He was incredibly clever. Everything I taught him he learned in an instant. He competed up to national level and became quite a well-known dog in his own right. There was a competition that tested the intelligence of your dog that finished with the finals at Crufts. Dill won and was crowned "DOG BRAIN OF BRITAIN".

Dill and I would then get invitations to prestigious events in London and around the country. It was fantastic for the Charity I still worked for as Dill and I were listed as being from Hearing Dogs.

There was nothing that Dill could not cope with and he loved every fresh challenge.

We had bought a cottage at a small village called Murcott in Oxfordshire. We had managed to buy it at a low cost for there had been some doubt about where the last link in the construction of the M40 was to go and the government had compulsorily purchased all the properties along the expected route. The route had been changed slightly so they were selling off properties and we purchased a house on the end of the village.

It needed work done on it but my Dad had taught me to be a child with practical skills amongst others and I loved working on it, painting, making it into a really homely cottage with a garden and a small stream that the dogs could be exercised and trained.

When the motorway was completed it was 3 fields away so prices of properties in Murcott began to recover and after a couple of years we were able to sell at a profit.

We immediately purchased a really dream house on lock 45 of the Grand Union Canal. You had to drive down a pathway to it. It was semi-detached Lock Keepers cottage, and was completely run down. The sitting tenant had died and British Waterways just wanted to sell it off.

Our canal-side cottage was for me a dream come true. It had rolling chalk hills behind and looked out on the Chiltern Hills. It so reminded me of my really happy childhood in Dorset.

I just couldn't believe it when our offer was accepted. It was absolutely perfect. It took a lot of work but we both loved doing it. All the plaster had to come off the walls, it needed a new damp-

proof course and it had woodworm. Here my former work in the building industry gave us the knowledge of what to do and we loved doing it.

We replaced or treated every piece of wood in the cottage, up ladders, scraping plaster off walls, painting the kitchen a carefully chosen pale lemon colour and by the time we finished it wasn't plush but it had all been done on a budget and it was heaven. It was absolutely perfect and the gardens were equally beautiful.

I was able to obtain some other animals. A local farmer had some lambs that needed bottle rearing and I would keep them in the house, and my joy of joys – we had eight ducklings in the kitchen.

Having painted the kitchen the ducklings habit of pooping in all directions – they could poo at right angles - did not help the décor but they were gorgeous – I absolutely loved them. I trained them to come when I called and to perform small tasks. I adored them but as they got a bit older we let them out. We lived next to the canal and once they were on the water it was *'cheerio Mum we're off to a life of our own'*. There was no way they would be shut in at night but they always came in the mornings for feeding. Then we got some doves; beautiful white doves – we put a dovecot on the back of the house and it was terrifically interesting watching them. Doves learn quickly because they have group behaviour and they would fly into the dovecot and sit and coo at you.

Our love of animals and our wish to communicate with all of them got us the nickname of *'Mr and Mrs Crazy'* amongst our neighbours. If I called on them and one of their children answered the door you could hear him call up to his mother *'Mum, Mrs Crazy's at the door'*

Life was as wonderful as it was possible to be.

I used to love going home and just being in my cottage with all my animals and my dogs. It was fantastic.

We had nearly 20 years of this idyllic living that I hoped would go on forever.

Years passed and I began to feel that I should begin a family. My fear of giving birth had receded and was being replaced by a desire to have a child of my own.

We tried for a while without success so I went to my GP for advice.

'Go away and keep trying for two years. If you are not pregnant after that time then come back and we will see what we can do.'

That was his total advice! Not at all helpful for we failed in our attempts over the next 2 years.

I was 39 years old when I went back to him!

We had one round of IVF but still I didn't get pregnant.

We thought we would like to get more into horse competitions so we decided we would sell this beautiful house – goodness knows why – it was probably the silliest decision we had ever made. The reason we did was that we had found a house – little semi – in a hamlet near Quainton. It had six or seven beautiful stables, an excellent and clean stable yard, kennels, a barn and about 5 acres. It was everything we would need for all our animals and the opportunity for the horses to be exercised and then hosed down in a yard instead of on thick mud.

We sold the canal cottage and made money on it with which we bought the house. It was perfect for us but for some reason as we first came into the house I had a gut feeling that we had done the wrong thing. We should never have sold canal cottage. We were happy there. Why did I feel the need for more?

We purchased new horses so that we could compete to an ever higher level but then began to discover the problems of working hard all day and then having to look after all the horses and animals on our return home after work. If one of the animals needed attention or the vet to call which of the two of us was going to lose time from work to be there? My husband had followed me up the promotions ladder at work so we were both in senior positions that required occasional time away from home. How do we manage all we need to do?

It all became more stressful than we had thought but we were able to do a lot more competing at week-ends with a lot of success. We did very well and then we bred some litters of puppies from our gun-dogs and I really enjoyed them. Besides training our own dogs I was also training dogs for other people.

We were managing well but then a job as Chief Executive Officer of the charity came up and we both knew it would have suited either of us perfectly. The message we were getting indicated that the managers would be happy for either of us to get the job.

However we were subsequently told -

'If we appoint a Chief Executive Officer from outside the charity then it is ok for you two to continue in your roles of Directors. If we appoint either of you then the other will have to leave the charity. We cannot have the two key roles occupied by 2 people in any sort of relationship'

Until that time there had been no word of appointing anyone from outside the organisation. The job was going to one or other of us.

Now conflict was in our marriage as we each wanted the job. I hesitated to apply for it as memories of the traumas in the early days of our marriage returned. I didn't know how my husband would react to the increase in stress our rivalry for the position would cause.

I didn't know what to do!

- Do I insist on staying and perhaps be the cause of my husband not getting the job?
- Do I renew my application for the CEO role on the grounds that it is usually easier for a male to land an equivalent role outside the organisation that it would be for a female?
- Do I leave the job I have filled so successfully for nearly 20 years and try to find another of equal standing?

It was all a dreadful dilemma for me and I wasn't sure how to handle it. Where does my life go from here?

When the decision was announced neither of us got the job!

They appointed someone from outside!

That result led to life at home and at work becoming really fraught. I was left with the feeling that my husband blamed me for him not getting the top job and my world was starting to collapse!

Thankfully I was still training other people's dogs and had started to research whether dogs could be trained to detect cancer.

I was still uncertain of what my future was to hold when events unfolded that were to fill me with terror and shock that is still with me all these years later.

***

Chapter Nine
South Korea

In the end I had settled on the only decision that was effectively open to me. I was to leave my job, take on the personal training of dogs, some consultancy work with other dog charities, and a day a week training cancer detection dogs

I would then also be able to oversee the work on our new canal cottage.

However I soon found that working for myself was vastly different from working for somebody else!

Resigning from a well-paid salaried job and replacing it with an income that fluctuated with one's ability to get another client is a very big shock to the system. I was used to a substantial cheque being paid into my bank each and every month now I was left wondering if I had enough cash in the bank for whatever purchase I was about to make.

I was picking up quite a lot of behavioural work on dogs and one day a week with Bucks NHS Trust trying to prove that dogs could

sniff cancer when we had a phone call from a lady from South Korea. She wanted someone who had managed an assistance dog programme to be seconded to South Korea for a number of months. She had heard that I was doing some consultancy work and that I was a behaviourist so it appeared that I fitted the bill.

She worked for Samsung, the electronics giant that employs nearly half the people in South Korea. They house a lot of their staff and they have a very big charitable arm that runs a zoo and supports an assistance dog training centre. The boss of Samsung is a dog owner and a dog lover with a drive to improve education in dog ownership.

South Korea has a very strong passion to be accepted into Western culture but one of the things that would always stop their acceptance in the West is their reputation for eating dogs.

The owner of Samsung had decided to put some money into educating the Korean public away from eating dogs and to a greater understanding and compatibility with animals.

They had started a South Korean Guide Dog organisation that had spread into other Assistance Dogs and then opened an Education Centre. Every week they would have visits from groups and schoolchildren, who they would educate to the fact that dogs were animals that could live alongside them, assist and help them, and give them a lot of love.

The Korean government supported this crusade by changing the law so that it was no longer acceptable to just go out on the street, pick up a stray dog, and take it home and eat it. Strangely this change of law had quite a severe downside as well as the obvious upside.

Samsung's boss put a lot of money into assistance dogs programme and they hired me as an independent contractor to visit South Korea for 3 or 4 months and hold seminars, lectures and help teach dog selection and training.

Off I went to South Korea for my first month. I had never worked on my own outside Europe before or away from home for any length of time and here was I on a 13 hour flight to a part of the world I knew little about. My uncertainty about the wisdom of my trip was compounded by the number of people who said –

'Oh blimey be careful Claire – they've got the Nuclear Bomb there and they are a very secretive lot.' [It was actually North Korea that had the Nuclear Bomb not South Korea. The South Koreans I met were lovely people open to Western culture]. Or they would say *'What on earth are you going there for Claire, they eat dogs!'*

I felt that if I didn't go then no-one was helping to try to educate the South Koreans to respect and train dogs. However almost nobody had anything positive to say about South Korea so I was quite apprehensive as we came into Seoul Airport.

To my surprise I found Seoul Airport to be as well constructed and as civilised as any western airport I had ever flown into. I was met by the lady who was bi-lingual and headed the assistance dog team. She drove us to the assistance dogs headquarters.

Life was very different in the countryside!

The first thing I noticed that at 6 feet in height I seemed incredibly tall when surrounded by the very much shorter South Koreans. I also noticed the absence of chairs and the problems I was having curling up my long frame to sit cross legged all the time.

I stayed most of the time at the Assistance Dog Centre or at week-ends at the house of one of the employees.

They had a Guide Dog Programme, a Hearing Dog Programme and a Detection Dog Program, so I started by lecturing to each group.

Their biggest problem was with Hearing Dogs.

They had 8 in training but they weren't functioning correctly. I quickly realised that the reason for their lack of success was because their trainers just hadn't seen the problems the dogs faced from the dog's point of view.

Koreans are accustomed to learning in a very different way than the English (they use learning by repetition – rout learning). I would give them a guide-line set of instructions that they could follow to train a dog but they would then follow them meticulously irrespective of the dog's reactions or temperament. In England a dog trainer would adapt your teachings to a way that suited them even when you did not want them to. In Korea after questioning each instruction and often over adapting and interfering with the dog's learning they followed the instructions they had written down meticulously even when the problems changed or the obstacle the dog had to overcome became scrambled or misplaced.

When I tried to point out that the changes would require slightly different instructions, out would come their notebooks *'But Miss Claire you said...'* and there would follow verbatim my instruction without consideration to how they might be applied to the changed circumstances. I rapidly had to adapt my training to their way of learning whilst continually trying to get them to see every problem or instruction through the dog's eyes.

The other great difficulty was actually empowering people to make decisions on dogs and adjust the training to suit the particular dog rather than carry out training instructions in the parrot-fashion way they had been taught at school.

They worked very long days and I was caught out when I was teaching them to map out a timetable of training. They couldn't understand all the white bits I had left by leaving Saturday and Sunday empty as week-ends and leaving gaps for holidays.

'What are the white bits? Why have you taken those days out?' they asked truly puzzled.

'Oh well that's when you have your holiday, and that's the week-end or Bank Holiday' I would explain.

'What do you mean, what is a week-end or Bank Holiday?'

'Well you have to take those out because you won't be here – you will be on holiday or away at a week-end'

'We don't have holidays, and often only get Sunday afternoon off.'

I began to appreciate how well off we are in the west.

There were two groups of assistance dogs and I lectured each group on behaviour and training.

The biggest problem I encountered was with the guide dogs and training them and their handlers to navigate the roads and through the markets. The markets had food scattered everywhere on the ground, pigs heads were stacked up alongside numerous stalls and training a dog and particularly a Labrador to pass and not eat the numerous raw meat temptations on route takes some doing.

When faced with multiple obstacles – a high curb, a car parked partly on the pavement, a canopy from the temporary stalls, the temporary stalls themselves; the dogs would stop but so would the handlers who had difficulty understanding why the dog had stopped and didn't know what command to give them. Everything would just shudder to a halt. They seemed to not understand why the dogs had stopped.

I explained that the dog could not see a way through that was safe for himself and the handler and thus would stop to enable a decision to be made. I explained and demonstrated how the dog needed support and assistance to make a decision of that complexity at that stage of its training or it would simply 'shut down'.

I helped them on ways to assess a dog and to choose those most suitable for training rather than just take hearing dogs out of the rescue centre on a first-in first-out principle irrespective of the dog's suitability to become an assistance dog.

The South Koreans were lovely people. They took me out on week-ends (Sunday afternoons) they allowed me to ride some of the Samsung horses from their outstanding show-jumping team, they made me feel very comfortable and

102

showed much appreciation of the way I was trying to help them

Amongst other ways Samsung was trying to educate South Koreans to appreciate animals was a zoo. Though I am generally against zoos this was put together in order to help children and their parents to appreciate animals, and to touch where possible and enjoy them. 'Samsung Everland' was rather like a Disney World paid for by Samsung and they ran the zoo.

South Koreans are trying to update their attitude to animals to match the views of the west but for hundreds of years dogs along with other animals have been seen as a source of food in the same way as the Western civilisations view lambs, pigs, chickens and cows etc. All of these are killed for food so it is difficult to condemn the Koreans for continuing with the practice of including dogs alongside all the farmyard animals much as I found the concept highly distressing.

There are hundreds of stray dogs in South Korea which have previously been seen as a free source of food. Picking them off the street and cooking them as you would a lamb or a goat effectively culled them. Now that eating stray dogs was forbidden they are rounded up and taken to a rescue centre.

I had no idea of this history and nothing prepared me for the horror of the centre bursting at the seams with unwanted dogs.

They housed 1,500 dogs in cages stacked high and exactly reminiscent of the battery chickens back home. Each dog had a cage of its own but only just big enough for it. Like our Battery Hens they were not taken out or exercised and with another 150 arriving each week the vet – who was a really lovely man – had no option other than to put down the 150 dogs each week that had been at the centre the longest.

He was hugely apologetic to me for this practice and begged me not to think too badly of them for it. He pointed out that there was no other alternative. They just could not accommodate any more and there was no hope of finding homes for all 1,500 stray dogs, a number that was increasing by 150 a week.

I tried to teach them how to assess the dogs. To choose those most suitable to be trained as assistance dogs but also how to define those that did not possess a temperament that would allow them to be a success if they were selected by a new owner coming to the rescue centre. Clearly the latter type of dog would be one chosen to be part of the cull whilst it was still necessary to put dogs down.

Traditionally dogs were culled on a time basis – first in – first out. Now at least those with the greatest chance of a successful life with a new owner had a chance of living long enough in the hope that such an owner could be found. Dog lovers did come to the Rescue Centre to adopt a dog to take home but before my training they were being given dogs that had been there longest but which might be totally unsuitable.

'No, don't give them that dog. It will be most unsuitable, give them this dog for all these reasons' was my common cry.

It was the first time workers at the centre had appreciated the requirement to match dog to owner.

I handled many dogs on my visits to the centre.

Assessed them with the staff, discussed the dog's attributes but then sadly had to return them to their cages from which they might never emerge again until they were culled.

The staff were always trying to get me to wear gloves when handling the dogs. *'No I can't wear gloves. I need to feel the strength of the dog, its heartbeat, its response to my touch and stroking, this can't be done in gloves!'*

And so days were spent lecturing and demonstrating as well as handling dogs to help their selection much more accurately than in the past

At the end of my stay in South Korea they were extremely grateful for all the advice I had given and for my efforts to increase their understanding and appreciation of animals and dogs.

'Please don't think badly of us,' said the Vet, *'we are very embarrassed by the reputation we have for eating dogs and we really are trying to address this.'*

'It is difficult. For hundreds of years dogs have been seen as a source of food alongside goats and lambs and other such animals. It is not easy to change that culture.'

They took me to an area where they had constructed a dog's grave. They were all extremely sad and gathered to say a little prayer for all the dogs they had been forced to put down. It was an extremely moving part of my stay.

The Vet turned to me -

'Please forgive me for what I have to do each and every day.'

It really was a terribly emotional moment for all of us.

The whole experience was moving! What tragedy humans cause when breeding pet dogs and not considering the long term implications. This is by no means a problem isolated to South Korea, but occurs all over the world! Through ignorance or economic considerations unwanted puppies – sometimes even pedigree dogs that have been bred for financial gain are culled when the breeders consider that it is no longer economic to keep them.

Was I helping them to change a Nation's traditional view of dogs and dog welfare? Were my efforts making any difference at all? That would be too much to expect but deep in my mind was the story about the little girl and the starfish washed up on the beach.

STARFISH

A young girl was walking along a beach upon which thousands of starfish had been washed up during a terrible storm. When she came to each starfish, she would pick it up, and throw it back into the ocean. People watched her with amusement.

She had been doing this for some time when a man approached her and said, "Little girl, why are you doing this? Look at this beach! You can't save all these starfish. You can't begin to make a difference!"

The girl seemed crushed, suddenly deflated. But after a few moments, she bent down, picked up another starfish, and hurled it as far as she could into the ocean. Then she looked up at the man and replied, "Well, I made a difference to that one!"

Claire Guest
"Listened to Daisy"

The old man looked at the girl inquisitively and thought about what she had done and said. Inspired, he joined the little girl in throwing starfish back into the sea. Soon others joined, and all the starfish were saved.

— Adapted from The Star Thrower by Loren C. Eiseley

This problem exists at many of the puppy farms in the UK. Often the puppies are bred then kept in terrible conditions only to be culled if they prove to be unwanted and yet we in the U.K. believe we are dog lovers. We are in no position to judge others, but the sadness we all can feel over the whole situation can be overwhelming, and I had to rapidly adapt my attitude so that I could continue to help them.

The vet had realised that I had not worn gloves. *'You have touched 150 dogs today and have not been bitten once. You have enough faith in what you do not to wear gloves despite the fact that we have rabies here'.*

My jaw dropped. I had not considered that some dogs might have been infected with rabies. I had not been bitten and not one dog scratched me because it was being aggressive but I had been scratched by some of the dog's claws as they desperately clung to me as I put them back in their cage.

A 13 hour flight home caused me to reflect on a month in South Korea. I came back with a different view on the world and on life.

I felt that I had done something really valuable. I felt I could help and reach far more people doing things like this. It also made me realise how lucky I was to have been born and live in a western country with all the privileges we have.

I also appreciated the wages I had earned. I felt it might just help and allow me to kick start the charity I was putting together to train dogs to 'sniff out' cancer.

I had contracted to go back in 6 weeks for my second session in South Korea. I was looking forward to it and the payment would give a further boost to my efforts in starting the charity.

On touching down at London Airport I was looking forward to getting home and back to my cottage and my husband. Sadly it led to the episodes that caused me such trauma that I do not feel capable of describing within the pages of this book.

It resulted in an emotional and nervous collapse that needed extremely urgent and skilled treatment to support and nurse me back to health.

I suffered severe Depression and Post-traumatic Stress which resulted amongst other symptoms in severe unpredictable Panic Attacks.

In the midst of this a call came from South Korea. They urgently needed me back for a few weeks to sort out some problem dogs they had and to supervise the training of some others.

My Psychiatrist was willing to let me go provided I meticulously took the medication he had prescribed and I phoned my Psychiatric Assessor every day at the appointed hour.

I think everyone hoped that the complete change of scene might help an otherwise lost soul.

Mum and Dad drove me to the airport then another calamity – I lost my passport. I had dropped it somewhere between the car and the check-in desk. It was another impossible position I had got myself into but as luck would have it a stranger had picked it up and got it back to me.

Mum and Dad waved me goodbye, goodness knows what was going through their minds and I checked-in. As I did so the events of the past few months welled up in me and I started to cry uncontrollably.

I continued to cry through the boarding lounge and onto the aircraft itself. Somehow I got upgraded to first-class where the seats converted into beds and I was able to immediately convert mine and cry myself to sleep. I woke up as we were coming into Seoul South Korea 13 hours later.

My clients picked me up at the airport and drove me to my accommodation. I was still heavily medicated and needed to sleep whenever I had a moment.

Interestingly I was able to assess the dogs and successfully work on curing their problems. I phoned my psychiatric assessor each day and slept in between my sessions with dogs and their trainers.

I returned home 3 weeks later still in absolute despair. Somehow through the mists I knew I was making life intolerable for everyone around me and I hated myself for it. If my parents had become unable to cope I would have to leave the home and care for me I would have absolutely nowhere to go apart from being sectioned in the psychiatric hospital.

Deep within me there was dawning the realisation that nobody could get me out of this psychological breakdown but myself. I had somehow to find a way out. The pain was so intense and kept returning. I knew there had to be some way to bring it to an end.

***

Chapter Ten
Recovery

There was no easy way back from the despair I had felt and though deeply depressed I found some comfort with my dogs and horses. I found that my animals not only provided huge love but were also fundamental in my recovery.

Every time I looked at Woody and how he coped so cheerfully with the problems he had how on earth could I feel so bad about myself and suicidal?

Woody really had no chance of survival. After birth he developed deformities that made it impossible for him to stand and get his mother's milk as his brothers and sisters did. His back legs were paralysed so badly that he had no right to stand let alone walk yet after sharing our love and training he would run up to me in the morning full of smiles and good cheer.

A vet who had seen him pronounced that *'There is no way that little dog could survive let alone walk yet I am watching him do precisely that.'*

Woody was as brave as a warrior and really loved life. I really loved that little dog. If he could achieve all he did - could I?

I still loved animals, music and driving and these were going to be my salvation. I was staying with my sister in Wendover and started to walk my dogs up into the Chiltern hills. The chalk hills of the Chilterns reminded me of Dorset and the happiness I had there as a child.

I would have Daisy at my side and Woody would walk where he could or be carried by me when the going was too tough for him. Dad would walk with me on occasions, sometimes I would be on my own except that the dogs were always with me. They slept on my bed. I don't think I would have managed without them. I had been nearly 20 years married and now there was this big empty bed – or there would have been but for the fact I had Daisy, Woody and Tangle snuggling back against me every night.

I used to ride whenever I could but my estranged husband came and took one of the horses to sell it set my recovery back a long way. However being out in nature and listening to the birdsong as I rode or walked started my wondering if nature provided the strength to give me some way through.

In Korea I had become very interested in Buddhism and Buddhist beliefs and mindfulness seemed to be a way forward. I felt I needed to concentrate my mind on the present. Not to consider what had happened in the past or what was going to happen in the future – just concentrate on the present.

I had brought back a number of meditation tapes and in the early days I would meditate for an hour or more nearly every day. I would meditate anywhere and everywhere. My favourite place for meditation was when alone with the dogs in the hills or out in nature.

I was lucky to be invited by a Canadian friend of mine to have a holiday with her in North Carolina where she was then living. I had a horrific journey. I was on anti-depressants but picked up an infection that needed anti-biotic. About two days before I travelled I started to get itchy skin that the doctor thought would wear off after a couple of days so off I went.

I had phoned my friend and warned her that I was suffering from acute depression and no longer the outgoing vigorous girl she had known but she insisted I visited and stayed with her as long as I needed.

'Claire – You've helped me through some difficult times in the past so get on the aircraft and come and stop with us for a couple of weeks at least'.

I left the family to look after the dogs and got on the flight. About 5 hours into it I suddenly thought that my face didn't feel right - the skin felt really tight. I turned to the lady sitting next to me –

'Excuse me – could you tell me if something has happened to me face?'

She looked at me and screamed saying *'You'd better call an Air Hostess'*

My face had swollen massively. The flight deck radioed a specialist doctor on the ground and a shot of adrenaline was considered but my breathing remained normal which was surprising as I had been suffering panic attacks for a long time.

As soon as I landed in Atlanta there was a medic waiting for me. He looked like a cowboy. He was wearing a Stetson hat, had on a check shirt and jeans and cowboy boots.

'Hey, what have you done to your face?' spoken in a broad Texan drawl.

'Nothing as far as I know'

'You have a bad allergy here. I'm going to stick something in your butt'

He injected me with cortisone and steroid and I had to have injections for the next few days. My friend was horrified when she saw me. She had known me as a vigorous girl who was as slim as a rake now she saw a hideously distorted Claire coming toward her.

Once over her shock she was very good about my appearance and good for me. We went riding every day and I used to sit out in the North Carolina countryside when she was out and practice the meditation. I did get very good at it.

I was waiting to start CBT (Cognitive Behaviour Therapy) and by the time I started that therapy I was able to meditate for an hour. I was in such deep meditation that it seemed like two minutes. I learned the way to stay in the moment and control my thoughts, not letting them drift back over the horrific events of the past.

I found it was the only way I could cope. Not thinking about the past not even the good times and also not thinking about the future. I was beginning to cope with my situation. When I got home I purchased a number of Buddha's and placed one in each room of my house.

They were all fine, elegant and beautiful, not as big as the huge Buddha's I had seen in the hills of Korea but very comforting to me every time I looked at them.

I started a hypnotherapy course at weekends and found I could lose myself in the studies and the intense physical pain I suffered from a stomach locked up with tension and stress would ease a little.

The course taught me that humans as well as dogs presented face to the world that might not truly reflect the person that was underneath it. If you could get past that face and understand the real person you could strip away the tension and often find a really pleasant soul.

I still had to find a way of easing the physical pain of knotted muscles that was always with me and some events, words or even sad music or songs could make that pain unbearable.

Dogs and horses have always had a huge part of my life but so has music. Were these the way to my salvation?

When I was young I used to love going to discos and dance to the music of the Bee Gees. I fell out of love with music when Disco moved into new romantic music in the 80s. I loved Soul and Disco music of the 70s. I found the beat very uplifting and enjoyed dancing to it. When in the despair of my depression I would go out and try to find tracks of the 70s even though I was clearly earmarked as an old eccentric by the 'dynamic' sales people in the record shops.

When I was in the early part of my depression I was just really surviving and I would occasionally hear a track on the radio that made me feel a little better but I never knew why.

My sister gave me a CD of the kind of music I had said I found lifted me and it was full of tracks that I thought were incredible. They were based on the way music had developed a genre called Soulful House that used Soul and Disco beats and puts them together in a modern form.

Any time slow romantic music was played as I was listening to the radio as I drove home I would instantly feel much worse and had to immediately switch the radio off. If they played House music I would immediately feel much better. It seemed to be a combination of the lyrics and the beat that lifted my soul.

Times were tough! My husband had left me with two horses but without any money to pay for the livery for one let alone two before he claimed one horse as his own and just came and took it.

I did not have enough income on my own to pay livery but Roger Mugford kindly offered to place my horse on his farm and invited me to visit whenever I wanted. I used to go to Roger's every other weekend. Thankfully the CD's I played in the car lifted my spirits and helped to alleviate the despair I felt at the position I had been left in. I survived by listening to this upbeat music all the time.

On one occasion Roger invited me to attend a conference in the Midlands and was picking up another passenger on route who was married to a producer of reggae music. She invited me to a party. I really wasn't mentally ready for a party and was still deeply depressed at the events that led up to the ending of my marriage.

'I really don't feel up to going to a party. They are full of people who are married and happy together whereas I am very much on my own and miserable'

'No do come. My husband has a lot of unmarried male friends and you might meet someone nice. You like dancing and there will be plenty of that'.

Somewhere along the way I had been told that the way towards a cure for acute depression was to accept all such invites so with much trepidation I accepted her invitation and went with her to the party. I love soul music and love to dance to it. At the party was a lovely looking West Indian man. He asked me to dance and I really wanted to say no but he was a great dancer and I got up and danced with him. I was soon able to lose myself in the music and the dancing. As the evening progressed he was chatting away to me.

'Claire, are you single/'
'Yes I am'

Claire Guest
"Listened to Daisy"

'Would you like to come out with me?'

'No. it's kind of you but I am not really into going out with anybody at the moment'

'Oh well no pressure, we can take it easy – go away for the week-end if you feel like it.'

'No, I'm really not up for that.'

However he persisted and at the end of the party my friend invited a group of us back to her place for drinks and coffee. Both of us were included.

'Are you coming back for coffee?' she asked him.

'Oh yes, I've got to persuade Claire to go out with me.'

Suddenly a voice came from somewhere behind us as we came down this long corridor leading out of the village hall.

'I don't think your wife would care for that much!'

He turned round to this voice and said something very rude to tell the voice to clear off and mind his own business but the voice repeated *'I don't think your wife will think much of that!'*

'Are you married?' I asked

'Oh well yes. But it's all remote and we are not really together'

'Oh yes you are' chimed the voice, *'and with four children!'*

The voice turned out to be a very genuine chap called Rob who was a carpenter and was another guest invited back to the house. At the house we had I started telling him about the disaster that was my house still stripped of all wood claddings from our eradication of dry rot that dated from before the break-up of my marriage. I was telling him that it was all contributing to the despair I felt with my life and he offered to call over a weekend and see if he could help put my beloved house back together.

'I've no money to pay you'.

'Don't worry, just provide me with a meal and I'll be happy to do what I can'.

'Oh I couldn't possibly let you do that'.

'Don't worry – I will be happy to fill my weekends when they are empty. I'll come and have a look and see if I can help. By the way do you like music?'

'I love music!'

He revealed that he was a DJ and from time to time played music at events all over the Midlands. I started to tell him how certain music lifted my spirits whilst other types could add to my depression. I accepted his kind offer to call and see if he could help.

Over many week-ends that followed he started reconstructing the rooms of my house one by one. He wouldn't take anything for his work but a meal. He seemed to enjoy using his skills to help. It was just like a weight had been removed from me. I was suffering severe depression made worse by the state of my house and over rooms that were chaotic, no floorboards or skirting, even no stairs. He would just sort it, rebuild all that needed replacing and room by room he was transforming the chaos into a lovely house again.

It turned out that he was an excellent DJ and the music he played was the upbeat music that I had found stimulating. He brought his record deck with him and played it loud whilst he worked. His music was a mixture of soul and disco and the House Music I so enjoyed.

Rob played music whilst he worked my spirits were lifted the whole time he was there.

Rob was dyslexic and left handed so had no confidence with reading or writing and had apparently been dismissed as thick by his teachers. He wrote much of his own music and couldn't explain

where his music came from but it seemed to me to come from some ethereal source. It was certainly tremendously uplifting and music was playing a huge role in my rehabilitation from the severe depression I had been suffering.

His music and his lyrics were beautiful and during the evening after work he would talk about them and explain why the various types of music affected my mood and my soul to such an extent. He would then play some disco music, some soul music and some of his own Soulful House music. He invited me to a boat party on the River Cam. The whole boat load of passengers danced all night to house music as the boat cruised along the River Cam. I absolutely loved it! My severe depression was never far away but apart from occasional relapses into it – my recovery was now well advanced.

My spirits had been lifted to such an extent that I started to pursue an idea I had been tinkering with for some time.

I had been working with the thoughts of forming a charity based on the cancer detection dogs I had been training since our British Medical Journal Publication in 2004.

I had been doing a lot of reading about how to form a charity but my Dad, bless him, whilst I had been in Korea had researched the multitude of requirements before the Charities Commission would register a new charity.

I had always been sure the way forward needed to be a charity. There weren't the certain financial returns to attract business to get involved and pay for all the steps ahead of us.

I wasn't sure that the successes I was certain we could achieve in the early detection of cancer and other life threatening deceases really belonged in the business sector.

Luckily John Church and my Dad shared that view and Dad being a solicitor was able to complete all the research and negotiations with the Charity Commissioners. Without his work we would never have been able to start up Medical Detection Dogs.

My Dad, John Church, Roger Mugford, Professor Daniel Mills, all agreed to be Trustees and I wanted a Chairman that I really respected and had the skills to be a relatively hard task master. I asked Michael Brander, Baron of Whittingehame. He was an entrepreneurial solicitor skilled at advising start-up companies. I knew him through his wife as we are both past chairs of the APBC - Association of Pet Behaviour Councillors. He accepted so we had an excellent Board to start the Charity.

At that time our Charity had two main sides – Bio-Detection; and Assistance Dogs.

I had already trained our first blood sugar detection dog.

When I came back from Carolina, USA I wanted to be sure I could train a diabetes dog and had got a phone call from a lady –

'I saw that you do cancer training. I wonder if you could help me? We are in a terrible state. We have walked guide dogs for many years but my husband has very brittle Type 1 diabetes. He is a lecturer at Durham University but we are wondering if he can carry on. He has monitored his blood sugars most of his life but he is now losing his awareness. He is collapsing most days. We need to call out

the Ambulance 2 or 3 times a week. He is collapsing at work and on his way to work. He used to go up through the allotment but I've found him unconscious there and he's been rushed into hospital. He is on Warfarin for another condition. I think he is not going to make it. He keeps falling over and hitting his head. Is there any way you could train a dog to help?

I told her *'I would like to help and would love the challenge but tell me about your dog. Does your dog show any signs that your husband is about to have an attack or that his blood sugars are low?*

'No she doesn't show anything!

They had a failed guide dog that they had homed

I arranged to go up and see the dog.

It was Valentines Day 2008. This was a terrible day for me, the pain caused by my depression was intense but luckily I had a 6 hour journey by car to get there so with the help of upbeat music playing on my car's CD player I was able to manage my emotions by the time I arrived.

I stayed with his family for 5 days. Her husband Cherry was having lots of hypo's and this intensified the training I was able to do with Zeta, their black Labrador. In that time we got her working.

I used the same techniques I had practiced on all the animals I had trained.

- watch the dog; don't interfere;
- look for behaviour light;
- look for what the dog is offering you
- it will be offering you something;
- when it does use the clicker
- reward to tell the dog you like that and reinforce its behaviour.

In Zeta's case she was offering something that they had not noticed – she would suddenly go very quiet. Within 6 weeks she was working reliably

So by the middle of 2008 I had my cancer dogs working reliably and now a diabetes dog successfully detecting and assisting.

My first cancer dogs Daisy and Tangle were being trained in my front room with urine samples kept in my freezer. I had to warn visitors not to make a mistake when they went to get a drink. There was only one room on my house that had not been completely gutted because of the dry rot so the dogs and I lived and trained in it.

The Buckinghamshire NHS Trust would supply samples from cancer wards and I would collect samples from non-cancer patients. I used to set the samples out on plates along the room and teach the dogs to sniff each and move on. When they detected a sample from a cancer patient they would sit in front of it and wait for the click and reward. They were remarkably accurate. Daisy has been measured at 93% accuracy which is way above many of the medical centres cancer detection techniques.

With cancer and diabetes dogs now trained we went ahead and applied for charitable status which after a hiccup was awarded by the Charities Commission in July 2008. Charity number 1124533.

There are many times I am reminded of the starfish story that helped me believe that I was making a difference in South Korea.

The same now applies to the work of the charity.

Gradually we may be able to achieve a number of centres around the country where medics can send urine samples for our dogs to screen.

I had no idea how long it would take to gain acceptance of our work and I wondered how many lives we could help save by the early detection of cancer or other life-threatening diseases?

***

Chapter Eleven
Medical Detection Dogs

The one room of my house that was capable of occupation had to serve as a training base as well as a living room. I trained the dogs with my sister Simone and at that time we had trained Zeta as a diabetes dog and Daisy, Tangle and Oak as cancer detection dogs.

At that time I used to set all the samples out on plates in a line and Mum and Dad loved to visit and watch the dogs go along the line until they detected a sample from a cancer patient. They would then sit in front of it waiting for the clicker and the reward.

We were ready to start the next cancer study. The BMJ study had been completed in 2004 and in 2008 we started a new study with Bucks NHS Trust looking at bigger sample sizes with results published in their Journal. This study took a long time and wasn't completed until 2011.

I recruited Rob Harris as a trainer in 2008 (what a good decision that was) and gave him cancer dog Oak. Simone was covering all the admin tasks and obtaining and preparing samples for testing and training the dogs.

Every spare moment of all of us was spent in Simone's conservatory writing to organisations trying to get support, sponsorship and donations that would allow us to get the charity up and running.

We got lots and lots of knockbacks! Many potential funders were considering our project and goals to be too much 'left of centre'; 'off the wall thinking' in their eyes to provide any funding but we did get some support and some believed in us. They shared our passion, enthusiasm and self-belief. Without these early supporters the charity would never have taken off.

With the new study that we were starting we needed a centre where we could train the dogs and measure their results. Carolyn Willis and I began to drive around the district until we found a disused building on Westcott Adventure Park about 4 miles west of Aylesbury which was very inexpensive. It had 3 small rooms, it was very wet, the roof leaked, it had single walls and was freezing cold but that is where the charity Medical Detection Dogs came into being under the name Cancer Bio-detection Dogs.

We got some funding from some generous Trusts that exist to support worthy causes and it was enough for us to fund our very early months. The money we had received from the hospital to pay for the study ran out long before it was completed but by that time we had managed to raise enough money from charitable trusts and donations to complete it.

By 2009 we were still writing letters to all and sundry seeking financial support and going to Foundations and making presentations. We were beginning to be offered dogs to train and managed to place one or two.

The depression had not left me but now I had a focus and a routine with a passion to succeed. The charity occupied much of my time and the severe depression was slowly coming under control.

I have been asked many times – did I think the charity would become such a success and the answer to that is Yes!

I did always think that the charity would succeed. I always felt that this whole thing was of such huge value that could touch people's lives and improve their quality of life.

Sometimes at night and when I was meditating I would get these visions of crowds of people smiling at me each with a dog in their Medical Detection red waistcoats.

I therefore had a vision of where the charity could go but the future frightened me whilst the past was still unbearable to think about.

I concentrated on living in the present not thinking of the past or considering the future and I received some excellent advice from one of my counsellors.

'Claire - promise me two things. No matter how depressed or suicidal you might feel when you wake up each morning you will say *to yourself 'I won't do anything today, it won't happen today!' Later you can extend that to 'it won't happen this week and then this month' but for now just say to yourself 'It won't happen today'*

'The second thing is - Don't concern yourself too much about what is going to happen in the future. The future will work out, don't try to think about 'if I do this or that then I can make that happen' the future will take care of itself.'

It was a very good piece of advice for it made me realise that I had spent all my life trying to reach this or that goal believing that if I could get there it would make me happy but discovering that when you get there it evaporates and you set another goal. *'If I get there I'll be happy'; get there and it evaporates! so you think ok let's get to another there and I'll be happy; and again it evaporates; then*

get there I'll be happy and there; and there; and every time as you reach your goal the happiness has evaporated!; and so you chase on with the happiness you were expecting as you reach every goal evaporating before your eyes.'

Meditating on this you realise that the object is to be happy today, never mind the past or future, if you are happy today then things will work out.

The Buddhist belief of staying in the present was really indicating the same thing. You are going along a path in life and things will happen to help you if you recognise them and let them.

I remember walking along the towpath of the canal one day and feeling terrible with an all-consuming emptiness – no house; no job; no husband; no joy!

The charity had just moved into the building at Westcott and we urgently needed some walls built to separate the building into a reception area where we could greet visitors, patients and potential sponsors, another room in which we could train the dogs, and a third that we could use for admin. We had no money to do any of this and our roof leaked, it was wet and freezing cold and all thoroughly depressing.

The task of the trainer is difficult enough without any interruption or distraction of visitors. The great secret of training the dogs is to wait for the dog to give you a signal that they have detected the odour caused by the disease or the oncoming attack and then to reinforce that action with a click and reward. The distraction caused by visitors in the same room interrupted the early training of the dog and trainer.

I sat on a bench feeling absolutely dreadful when I got a phone call from Richard at the Bucks Herald.

Hello Claire, I hear you have set up a charity. Why don't you come over and see me.'

I did and the Bucks Herald ran an article on us and outlined some of our urgent needs. When the article was published I got a call from a local carpenter/joiner offering to build the walls at no cost to us. He did and it was another lesson on not getting too concerned for the future but to be happy today.

All kinds of volunteers came in to help us and I began to realise that kindness is amongst us all the time – in huge amounts! Often we cannot see it or we even block it out of our vision as we process the bad things that have happened to us – but kindness is

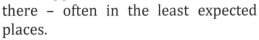

there – often in the least expected places.

It was at Westcott that we set up the carousel. Using plates on the floor was backbreaking for Rob and I and the carousel had the added advantage of being capable of being spun before the dogs came in the room so that visitors could see that the trainer would not know where the cancer sample was and influence the dog accordingly.

The message the dogs gave me came

from the way they enjoyed the day. They are cognoscente of the past but don't fret over the future, it will take care of itself. Woody enjoyed every day and every challenge

We were at Westcott from April 2008 to November 2011.

I had started going out with my DJ and listening to his knowledge of music I resolved never to listen to the slow beat love songs that were having such a depressing effect on me but to concentrate on his upbeat Soulful House music.

We spent a lovely holiday in a caravan in Dorset, bought a couple of really tasty looking Cornish Pasties, put them on one side while we took the dogs for a walk on the beach. I was holding the string of a kite that Rob had bought and was flying happily when a sharp gust of wind caused the cord to slip from my grasp and the kite to take off. Rob went rushing after it hollering at it to stop much to the amusement of everyone on the beach but as soon as he managed to grab the cord a gust of wind caused it to again slip from his grasp and continued flying out over the sea. He was still chasing it as the water was getting deeper and slowing him down so he dived full length and swam after the cord forgetting he was still fully clothed. He was making so much noise everybody on the beach was entertained. Each plunge nearly got the chord but the

wind would just whisk it out of Rob's hand at the last moment. When he finally gave up and stood up he was waist deep in the sea as he watched his beloved kite soaring over the waves and across the bay. It was a fully clothed Rob, soaked from head to foot – without his kite, that emerged from the sea with the whole beach in stitches.

In all the excitement we had not noticed that one of our dogs was missing. We called and looked around but no sign of Woody.

124

We got back to the caravan for Rob to change into some dry clothes to find Woody sitting in the remains of two lovely Dorset pasties with only the crumbs remaining.

Rob's cry of; *'The little Fokker! He's eaten our pasties,'* was heard all over the beach. From then on Woody had a pet name of *'The little Fokker!'* I have to say it did rather suit him.

I was on my own with the dogs in Lincolnshire and after a meeting with a friend to revise for a hypotherapy exam I decided to take the dogs to have a run on the beach I found a parking place, opened the boot of the car, out jumped Tangle and Woody but Daisy didn't go with them as is her usual custom.

Instead Daisy pushed into me nudged me and looked anxiously at me with her big eyes..

'What are you doing Daisy? Get out of the car!'

But she wouldn't, she still pushed into me. It was painful and this was totally foreign to her normal behaviour. What on earth was wrong with her?

I eventually got her out of the car and down to the beach. She didn't repeat this behaviour but that evening I realised that she had bruised me. My chest was sore and as I rubbed it I thought I could detect a lump that I had not known existed! Next morning the lump was still there! I told my sister about it.

'Claire; go and get it checked out. Don't fret about it most of these lumps turn out to be cysts but go and get it checked out today.'

I went to the doctor but I could see from her face she was not very happy about it.

'I am going to refer you straight away; you will be seen within 2 weeks.'

'Look I'm really busy and I've got piles of medicines and I'm going away so I don't think I can attend a clinic'.

I was not given any choice and was referred within 2 days to see a very eminent breast surgeon.

'I'm pretty sure it is a cyst but I'm going to put a needle into it for you'.

He put two needles in it and it was excruciatingly painful. He sent me for a mammogram a day or so later. When the results were through he said -

'We've done your biopsy. The results are clear but there is something a little bit concerning on your mammogram. It is much deeper than this lump. I don't want to overplay the problem as they often turn out all right but I do want you to go onto some core biopsy in a special unit.'

It appeared it was going to be a very deep core biopsy and though the specialist put as much local anaesthetic as he could it was extremely painful.

When I came out from it the nurse said *'you've been in there a long time; 45 minutes, I think he didn't want to miss anything.'*

I got called back a few days later to get the results; Mum and Dad were not available so my new boyfriend – my DJ who had been re furbishing my house and given Woody a new nickname - drove me there.

The specialist came in the room with a nurse who sat beside him. I remembered someone telling me that if they have a nurse sat with you when they break the news then it is Cancer.

'I'm sorry to tell you we have found cancer. We have found it early and we will be operating as soon as possible and following with a course of radio therapy and depending on whether we have been successful with clearing the core in the operation we may follow with chemotherapy.'

My boyfriend was gasping for air as the specialist detailed out his findings but I was calm. I had been through so much acute depression over the past few years it seemed to me to be just a continuation of the way my life was moving.

I was operated on within days.

'You have been incredibly lucky! The cancer was so deep that had you not come in for a check-up we would never have found it until it was far too late.'

I suddenly realised that I had only gone for a check-up because Daisy had nudged my chest and wouldn't get out of the car, just continually nudging my chest and causing me to rub away the bruising I thought she had caused.

I remembered Daisy's face and realised she was warning me. I had taught her to sniff out cancer in urine samples since she was 12 weeks old, could it be that she had somehow detected a cancer within my chest. Certainly her actions were commensurate with exactly that conclusion.

I had radiotherapy 5 days a week for 6 weeks at Mount Vernon Hospital where I met the lovely Alan Makepeace who was to become an oncologist advisor at Medical Detection Dogs.

He was delightful from the moment I walked into see him and has remained so throughout our work together at the charity. He is such a gentle person. My surgeon and my oncologist are now both advisors to the charity.

One of our trustees at the Charity is Betsy Duncan Smith who has also suffered cancer. She did not have the advantage of a dog warning her that she had cancer and thus did not have an early diagnosis. Her treatment was tough and she wanted to recover and get back to normal. As a consequence she did not want to come along to one of our demonstrations when she first heard of the charity. However come she did and once she saw what the dogs can do to give early and accurate warning of cancer in a sample or a patient she has become one of most enthusiastic supporters and trustees.

She came at a time that we were getting a huge amount of scepticism from the medical specialists, government officials, cancer charities and a great deal of the media. Most of these completely ignored my invitations to come along to one of our demonstrations and see our dogs working.

I often felt that I was banging my head against a brick wall as we tried to get the charity going. It was only the enthusiasm and support of a close family of relatives, friends, a few full time helpers and people like Betsy that gave me hope that we could break through the inertia of the established views of how to detect cancer

At that time the deep radiotherapy it was burning a lot of my skin. Coming into the freezing cold and damp rooms at Westcott was no fun whatsoever. Funds were coming in from the generous donors and trusts and we had enough funding to think about a move to accommodation that better suited us and the increased activity we were experiencing in the new charity.

Driving for weeks and weeks to hospital and back for my daily radiotherapy session gave me lots of time to reflect, the impact of what Daisy had done for me was becoming more real.

I was a lucky one, Daisy had drawn my attention to my cancer so early that I had confirmation that I would not require chemotherapy. The radiotherapy was an arduous process and sore but I did not experience all the hair loss and other side effects that chemotherapy would have given me. Daisy had warned me when my cancer was at an early grade and stage, this is what I had hoped that our work would do for 1000's of people in the future, to save lives. It had happened to me at a time when I wondered with all the scepticism whether the cancer detection work would continue.

At times I felt sorry for myself, my estranged husband did nothing but continue his cold aggression and I wondered why I had cancer to add to list of things to deal with, but it could not be ignored, Daisy had saved my life through her early warning. How many other lives could this knowledge save in the future? How many friends, relatives and love ones have been lost because of late diagnosis?

In the UK we have one of the worst survival rates for cancer. This is due not to poor treatment but to late diagnosis.

Our work at Medical Detection Dogs could not be ignored. It was a stark reminder that I had to continue. Daisy's message was clear - but first I must recover from my emotional and nervous collapse.

I started learning Tai Chi

The demonstrations of the instructor convinced me that physical strength and energy were very closely related to one's mental state. He got me pushing my arm up against his pressure to lower it whilst thinking of my recent past and though I swear I was pushing as hard as I could my arm dropped rapidly under his pressure. I was then made to think about the nicest thing that had happened to me in the present and he found it extremely difficult to force my arm down.

It was another lesson on why I should stay in the present and live life one day at a time. It really made me realise how my internal thoughts were affecting my physical wellbeing and energy. He also demonstrated how energy can be transferred from one to another with or without physical contact.

Tai Chi following on from my acquaintance with Buddhism in Korea and my deep meditation finally brought home to me the ways I can avoid letting energy seep away from the body. I still take on too much but hope I can now recognise the symptoms and can step back and delegate some of the tasks.

One task I did get involved in was the search for new premises for the charity. We were getting more and more people coming to us to discuss their needs and problems to see if the dogs could be trained to help and they were coming into the cold damp building at Westcott.

We had managed to get a grant that would pay the rent on better premises for a few years and set out in search all around the area. As soon as I saw number 3 Millfield on the Greenway Business Park at Great Horwood in Buckinghamshire I knew it was the place. It fitted so perfectly the vision I had often had of entering a building to see hundreds of smiling faces with dogs wearing the red waistcoats of Medical Detection Dogs.

We could afford the rent of number 3 but who knows perhaps numbers 1 and 2 might also become available at some time in the future. Stay in the present and kit out number 3 to serve all we needed to do today.

We began to get ever more interest in our work and began to receive grants to help us. It allowed us to set up the study of the work of the dogs.

Unfortunately the people we were working with on the study were not dog trainers but were analysts and would not reveal to us which samples were cancerous thus we were unable to reward correct diagnosis by the dog who became in danger of wondering exactly what it was expected to do.

The statisticians and medics wouldn't or couldn't give us immediate results so we had no way of knowing if the result was right or wrong and no way of reinforcing the training of the dog. Without rewarding the dog each time it achieved a successful detection the dog doesn't have any reinforcement that it is doing what is wanted. It is only the quality of the training we had given them prior to the tests that allowed them to seek the cancerous sample.

The longer the tests continued the less certain the dogs became that they were doing the right thing. We couldn't help them as the statisticians were unable to tell us if the dog had got it right or wrong in time for a reward and a click to be given. This was frustrating and beginning to distort results and was one of the reasons why the study dragged on until 2011. Our dogs were becoming confused and their performance was deteriorating.

It was all so depressing that I began to wonder if we should drop the cancer detection side of the charity and concentrate on the diabetes and other life threatening disease detection and assistance. However results from around the world were showing very positive results and this and visits and support from some very influential people in medical research kept us going with

Cancer Detection. They helped to convince us that we were doing very valuable work that would have a very positive result so we must keep going. We did but we were very relieved when the second study was complete.

The study showed that the dogs could detect Cancer at high level of accuracy, the best dog at 73% though we were all convinced their scores would have been much higher had we been able to reward the dog after each test.

Thankfully today we have electronic monitoring and are blessed with an excellent statistician who is evaluating our work so results come out promptly and accurately and the dog's training is enhanced. Daisy has been measured with 93% accuracy at detecting Bladder and Prostate cancer.

As time passes I am getting more and more days where I wake up thinking *'You know, there are quite a lot of things I will enjoy doing today'* rather than the dark thoughts that blighted my life for so long after the terrifying days at the end of my marriage.

Getting funding to continue the charity has always been a struggle but somehow funds arrived just as we needed them. The thing that really drove us on was the certainty that our trained dogs could do so much to improve or even save the lives of so many people.

A very sad tale from a lady recently revealed that her husband had been in hospital for just over 3 weeks being treated for Prostate Cancer. She no sooner got him home when the hospital phoned up to get him back up for further tests. These revealed that he had Pancreatic Cancer and just 3 weeks to live. The hospital explained that the test for Prostate and Pancreatic Cancer differs and testing for one would not reveal the other.

We are certain that a dog's nose would reveal the two cancers from the urine tests. We further believe the dog can detect either cancer by smell from the breath of the patient. There is still much testing to be done in this area but I do get frustrated at the rejection of so many in the medical profession and some of the cancer charities.

Just think how a dog could now have given that lady a so much better chance of still enjoying the company of her husband by early diagnosis that sadly was missed by the medical profession.

There is interest in a move to build an electronic nose that imitates the nose of a dog. Whether they will ever succeed I cannot tell but the hugely encouraging thing is that all the effort and money spent on this project is a clear acceptance that a dog can sniff out cancer and other life threatening deceases.

I can't help thinking of the enormous costs associated with attempting to build an electronic dog's nose when there are real dog's noses ready and available. If this amount of money and effort were to be spent on a series of Medical Detection Centres around the country to which local health centres could send urine samples of patients they suspect might have cancer it would allow early detection and save a huge number of people's lives. It would also save the NHS budget a huge amount of money!

Chapter Twelve
Dogs detecting Cancer and other Diseases

Dogs must have been trying to warn humans of the presence of illnesses and diseases for hundreds of years but with few exceptions we failed to listen to them. It's not clear why dogs should be so good at doing this but the evidence shows that they are.

Anecdotal evidence indicated that a number of people who had a close bond with their dog had understood the dog trying to signal that something was amiss but there was little evidence that the dogs traced the disease by smell.

My friend Gillian had described the way her dog would keep alerting her to a melanoma on her leg by sniffing the air each time she passed and following her until it could lick the affected area or press its nose against the spot through any trousers or leggings she was wearing. The way Gillian described it her dog even when sleeping would lift its head and sniff as she passed. It was immediately apparent to me that the dog was using its nose to detect the skin cancer.

At that time Gill and I believed that it was a change in the cell construction of the melanoma that the dog could smell. We both got very enthusiastic about trying to prove that dogs could smell cancer but had no means of proving it.

At that time the eminent surgeon John Church was experimenting with using maggots to heal wounds. He had heard a number of stories from owners whose dogs had warned them of the presence of disease in their bodies and though he did not at that time own a dog he recalled that he was always aware of Typhoid on a ward when doing his rounds by the smell as he entered the ward. If he could smell Typhoid what could a dog's much more powerful sense of smell detect? He posed the question that if a person had a tumour on his bladder would this drop cells into their urine and thus release the volatiles (VOC's) known as 'smelly compounds' that can be detected from their urine.

Gill worked with me at Hearing Dogs and rushed in one day imploring me to switch onto Radio 4 where John Church was talking about his theory that dogs could detect cancer and inviting listeners to get in touch if they had any similar stories.

'Claire this is the first time we have heard of a medical professional who holds the same belief as us. We must contact him straight away.'

A phone call to Radio 4 got us put through to him and we discovered that we all lived within 20 minutes of each other so met up that same evening. Our meeting excited all three of us and we became determined to set up a way of proving our theories.

There were organisations in various parts of the world who were already working on the theory and in 2002 we contacted them all with a proposal that we hold a symposium that would discuss whether or not dogs could detect illness or disease and how we research it.

The symposium was well attended with many delegates travelling from various parts of the world. Pine Street Clinic in California had done some early work on detecting Breast Cancer and came over for the symposium and a number of prominent others attended.

There was enough belief in the room and anecdotal evidence from everybody's early work in this field to make us determined to test out the premise that dogs could detect cancer.

The various groups went about their attempts to prove the premise in very different ways and set up a variety of tests and trials. We looked at some of these and concluded that care needed to be taken in the way the tests were set up to ensure they did not favour the dog or would be biased in a way that might improve the results and give a false reading. The greatest care we needed to take was to ensure the way that urine samples of non-cancer and of cancer patients were used.

When they were 'sniffed' they must not allow the dogs to use their other senses – sight, consistent positioning of the cancer sample, reaction of the trainer, and so on to define the cancer sample. John Church was coming at the question from the medical side we were coming at the same question from the training side.

John had reported a dozen or so anecdotal stories of dogs smelling cancer, most concerned melanomas, one concerned breast cancer and one was a tumour on a colon. These had been published in a letter to the 'Lancet' medical journal in 1998..

Melanomas appear on the skin and can be detected by sight. We needed to establish whether dogs could smell an internal cancer and how reliable was its detection.

We formed a group to take this forward which included; John Church, representatives and medics from Bucks NHS Trust, Gill and myself and we met regularly to work out how we would go about this task.

We lined a series of urine samples up in a line of plates from non-cancer and cancerous patients. When Tangle and other dogs we had training began to show an interest in what we were asking them to do and looked as though they was actually detecting something in the cancer samples it was so exciting.

One of my passions is to empower the dog to tell us what knows. We don't know what the dog can detect or is trying to communicate to us – we must listen to and watch the dog to try to interpret early signals.

You must teach the dog to become a problem solver.

One of the ways of doing this is to start on something relatively simple like sniffing an Earl Grey tea bag and teaching the dog to sit in front of it, giving the dog a click on the clicker and a reward every time it does so. You can then put a number of samples down under covers only one of which is a teabag. When the dog sniffs it and sits in front of it you give it a click and reward. You can then put other makes of teabags under the other covers and click and reward each time the dog sits in front of the Earl Grey and stares at it. Once the dogs have learned this game then you can use the dogs problem solving skills on other items until they move up to samples of human urine and you click and reward when it sits in front of and stares at the cancer sample.

The dogs can become so skilled at this that they can whistle past healthy samples and sit and stare at cancerous ones. When cancer affects somebody or when we get toward old age a number of changes occur in the body, we now believe that each or many of the changes give off an odour so the dog may be sniffing a multitude of odours from which we are asking it to detect the one that indicates cancer. The fact that our top dog has been measured with 93% accuracy at detecting cancer just shows how incredible their abilities are.

One of the keys to our testing was to profile the person giving the sample. Thus all the samples used in a particular test came from people of similar age and background. Our dogs will whiz past samples taken from young and fit people as they give little or no odour. They will linger over samples taken from old people as though they are *seeking to spot the red flower in a Monet painting* that indicates Cancer is present amongst the fog of odours the older body is generating.

Another key to success is that once you have trained the dog and know it can successfully make the decision and detect the cancer samples then you must trust it to do so. An example of this occurred when we were confident that Tangle could detect cancer and were setting up an important trial to prove it with Carolyn Willis from the Bucks NHS Trust. Carolyn was a hard task master – quite rightly – for she wanted to get the results published. This test was to be the pivotal trial that was published in the British Medical Journal.

We set out the samples and Tangle went straight up to the first, sat upright in front of it and started hard at it. Now we believed that it was from a healthy patient that did not have cancer so there was no click and reward for Tangle much to the dog's disgust. I set the test up again and Tangle did exactly the same again. Again no click and reward and Tangle's expression was clearly showing that he was now completely puzzled about what we were expecting him to do.

We aborted the trial declaring it a failure to our great disappointment. A few weeks later we had an eminent urologist come to see our work and he was very encouraging. He asked how reliable the dogs were and at that time we had about a 75% accuracy rate during their training but that one sample was giving our dog particular difficulties.

'In what way?' he asked?

I had got another sample from the gentleman in question and placed it in the line. Tangle reacted in exactly the same way again.

'Could look at the names of the people whose samples you have been using, some of them might be my patients?'

The tests are set up so that the identity of the person providing the sample is completely unknown to us. The sample is only identified by a coded number. Because these were his patients we were allowed to give him the code name of the samples used that day.

It appeared that the codes were allocated to samples supplied by his department and there were a number of his patients amongst them including the one that had so confused Tangle and led to us aborting the trial.

He had personally tested and cleared that patient for bladder cancer.. However impressed by the work of our dogs he recalled that patient and was kind enough to contact us a week or so later.

You might be interested to know that I recalled that patient back. I was so impressed by your dog that I thought I should do further tests and we have found that that particular patient has a tumour on his kidney!'

The earlier medical tests performed for Bladder Cancer had failed to detect the Cancer in the Kidney but Tangle was certain it was present.

From that moment on I just knew that the dogs could do it.

Dogs could detect Cancer.

It was a lesson to us to trust the dog to make a decision and not to conclude that the dog is wrong until all the facts had been gathered and corrected. It took a number of weeks before Tangle got over his confusion and begin to perform at top pitch again.

I used the sample again with others in front of him and again he sat in front of it and stared at it. This time it was a click and reward and he looked at me as if to say *'Well it's about time, I've been telling you for weeks that this patient has cancer and at long last you believe me!'*

Bless his little heart – he rapidly forgave me for confusing him and now he was certain what I was asking from him he was soon back to full efficiency.

The accepted concept at that time was that we had to teach the dog what the odour of cancer smelt like and then put samples in front of it to see if it could detect that odour. The problem was that we didn't know if Breast Cancer smelt any different from Bowel Cancer or from Prostate Cancer or from any other cancer. If we teach the dog to detect one cancer would it miss others?

To me at this time this was all being too specific. I believed that from our training dogs were intelligent enough to work out that a cancer ingredient was present and indicate by sitting and staring. We might be able to refine our training so that dogs sniffed out a particular cancer but our first objective was to prove dogs could detect cancer. If we proved that then the implications for early and inexpensive diagnosis of cancer were dramatic. The type of cancer detection could follow.

Tangle was only 6 months old when he began to reveal to us that there was an ingredient in the urine of cancer patients that he could detect and signal to us.

I almost couldn't believe it myself despite my early confidence. Most of the training was done in my Mum and Dad's kitchen and I would get my friends in and implore them to *'Watch this, it's incredible. Tangle is sniffing urine samples and telling us which patients are suffering from cancer!'*

As I accepted that Tangle was getting to be extremely efficient at detecting cancer I knew my next problems would be finding enough samples to use in testing and training from patients from all ages with profiles that accurately defined their disease within a variety of other diseases and conditions to act as a cancer free but diseased controls.

We would then need to recruit and train enough trainers to teach the dogs.

If we could achieve that and get medical and public acceptance of our work I could visualise a number of these centres around the country that GPs and consultants could send urine samples to for testing and perhaps giving early detection of cancers. They would certainly give the medical professionals a second opinion that would be inexpensive to use and still would not stop them from undertaking the medical tests they would normally instigate.

In fact it would support other tests providing valuable additional information to improve diagnosis. The current test for Prostate cancer – the PSA blood test - has a 75% false positive rate.

Three out of every four men tested using the PSV blood test will have a false positive reading indicating that they have Cancer when in fact they do not.

The biopsy that follows is painful and invasive and has a false negative of 30%. This means that one man in three will be sent home as cancer free when in fact he has Cancer!

What a difference a non-invasive urine 'dog test' could make – it is immensely more accurate and currently has a low false positive rate (under 10%) and accuracy of over 90%

The clinician could use this information to make a diagnosis. The dog assists the doctor and does not as the media sometimes incorrectly claim 'become the doctor'.

For those who are dog lovers the impact of this possibility is immediately seen but now the message is being seen by the many. Dogs can save lives!

My experience has shown me that many dogs can be trained by medical detection dogs to do this with great efficiency.

The dogs can define a healthy patient by walking straight past a sample and showing no interest in but will pause on the sample from an unhealthy patient whist it defines whether cancer is present. The implications of this are enormous!

An unhealthy sample may contain ingredients from any number of complaints so inexpensive and efficient early detection of a multitude of diseases and complaints becomes possible.

Could an annual submission of a urine sample to a Medical Detection Centre prove to be a reliable and inexpensive health check?

If the answer to that is yes then there could be massive savings to the ever burgeoning medical health budgets of every country in the world. The possibilities are mind blowing but first there is the job of getting the charity set up so that we can continue this work and take it to whatever levels of medical detection and assistance prove to be possible.

Can you imagine our feelings as we started the testing of dogs to detect cancer?

THE CANCER DETECTION DOG STORY
Introducing the dogs
(This extract was written in 2004 and is included to give the reader an understanding of the early days of the dogs detecting cancer).

It was Tangle who first caused the hairs to rise on the backs of our necks on that memorable summer's day in 2002.

We all just looked at each other in disbelief as this laid back little spaniel sniffed up and down the line of patients' urine samples and calmly picked out the one that had been given by a cancer patient, even though he had never met any of the people involved.

It was as if he were party to the very secret of life and death itself. Completely oblivious to the stunned reaction he had caused in his human audience, he wondered why no-one would give him the treat that he so obviously deserved.

The truth is, we were in a state of shock. Despite the fact that all the previous stages of training had gone so well – and Tangle was our most reliable dog – we had not dared to believe that the dogs would really be able to tell the difference between those half millilitre samples that had been given by patients with cancer as opposed to those given by patients with other diseases.

Yet Tangle had just shown us that the theory was in fact a reality: dogs could be trained to detect cancer...or at least one dog could, anyway.

Now it was the turn of others in the doggy team to attempt the same test. -

Biddy,
Eliza,
Reef,
Bee,
Toddy,
Jade and
Tich

But of course I'm getting ahead of myself.

The moment of truth when Tangle shocked us into stunned silence was the culmination of several months of training, with many dogs and dog-trainers involved.

We must jump back in time to April 6th, 2002, the day when our very first cancer sample arrived.

The room was filled with an expectant hum of excitement and the distinctive smell of warm wet dogs... this was the weekly get-together of the cancer detection dog team. Up until this point we had all been introducing the idea of scent-discrimination to our dogs with various weird and wonderful exercises.

For example,

Reef, the somewhat gangly wire-haired pointer puppy, had become expert at distinguishing Earl Grey teabags from common old PG Tips;

Titch, on the other hand, (so-called because of her small but perfectly formed Jack Russell Terrier frame which put her at the approximate eye-level of a bee's knee) was more of a fruit sort of person, having developed a penchant for differentiating those flower pots which hid oranges from those that covered up apples.

So desperate had we been to make progress with our dogs while we waited impatiently for our first cancer samples to arrive that we had seen any manner of scented objects as fair game for our training purposes.

Of course, we were well aware that our labours could be in vain as there was always the risk that we were doing more harm than good! After all, keying our dogs into tea bags and oranges might teach them something useful regarding the overall concept of scent-discrimination, but what if their first love of oranges proved stronger than any subsequent key scent such as cancer? What if they failed to make the necessary transition?

Luckily for us, April 6th soon arrived, and with it our very first cancer sample.

The room went still as Carolyn came in with her white coat and her coolbox.

Silent, apart from the sound of playful growls as Reef tried to fit Eliza's head into his mouth, something which was eminently possible, he a German Wire Haired Pointer, she a diminutive Papillon.

Eliza, a sensible seven year old, could not see the point of becoming a German Pointer's dinner, and sharply told the young upstart to stop fooling around; after all everyone else in the room had fallen silent and was listening intently to every word that Carolyn said-

There were procedures to be explained and protocols to be learned by heart.

Surgical gloves must be worn whenever handling samples.

These were to be changed every time a different sample was touched as scent could so easily be transferred from one sample to another.

No woman who was either pregnant or intending to become pregnant could touch any sample (not because of any risks associated with cancer cells themselves but rather because of the chance of the urine containing various viruses, the cytomegalovirus virus in particular).

Any woman falling into this category should retire from the team now. Our eyes moved furtively around the room and the tension was something akin to that moment in a marriage ceremony when anyone knowing of any just impediment should declare it now...but no-one did.

Vets had been consulted and could see no reason to suspect risks to the dogs from coming into contact with the urine, after all, this was what dogs had done day in day out for thousands of years.

Samples were frozen down to minus 35 degrees centigrade.

We were all transfixed by the sight of our first sample.

The ice on the glass vial concealed the yellowish substance within. A contribution willingly given by someone who knew their life was nearing the end but who hoped to help our team make crucial advances in the fight against cancer – a fight that would continue well after their death.

We resolved never to lose sight of the fact that these glass vials contained more than just urine samples, but the hopes and fears of real people. We owed it to them to give it our very best shot.

Carolyn's instructions were typed up and passed round. And then we were ready to begin training our dogs in earnest.

The dogs we were training were a mixed bunch. Young and old; pedigree and mongrel; big and small.

I should explain that these dogs were all pets.

As events unfolded the numbers of trainers in the team dwindled to just the four of us as others found the additional hours too onerous, or their dogs missed vital training because of this.

But again, we are jumping ahead of ourselves.

Back in April 2002 we started out with our first cancer samples and five trainers waiting to put on their surgical gloves for the first time.

Focussing for a minute on the two-legged members of the group assembled in the room, we were all professional dog trainers who transformed rescued and abandoned dogs into working Assistance Dogs on a daily basis, but we also brought other skills into the melting pot too.

Some of us were competitive Gundog trainers in our spare time, others were successful Working Trial and Obedience competitors.

As for the four-legged side of the equation, although all of the dogs knew basic obedience commands very few of them had been trained specifically for scent-related exercises.

We deliberately wished to start with dogs that were representative of dogdom itself, rather than an elite subsection of specially picked "scent experts" – after all, this was a Proof of Principle Study to see if dogs could be trained to detect cancer.

We all suspected that the best dogs for the job would be those breeds typically associated with the working disciplines, but we wished to make no assumptions at this stage.

And so it was that the original band of dogs consisted of –

a German Wire-Haired Pointer,
a Labrador,
a Jack Russell Terrier,
two Cocker Spaniels,
a Mongrel,
and a Papillon.

Before the story is told, let's meet them.

Eliza, a 7 year old female Papillion (butterfly dog).
Bags of attitude in a miniature body. Could Eliza surprise the sceptics by showing that a toy breed could do the job as well as the more traditional working breeds?

Titch, a 2 year old female Jack Russell Terrier,
Originally abandoned and taken into a rescue centre. Could she change her focus from Citrus fruit to something much more sinister?

Biddy a tiny 2 year old chocolate coloured working cocker.
Bred in Scotland as a working spaniel to assist in the shooting field and find game. With legs not much longer than Titch, she was to take her work seriously.

Reef, A 10 month old male German Wire-Haired Pointer puppy.
Under training for agility competitions. Would Reef smell cancer as accurately as tea bags (on which he was perfect...)?

Jade, 7 year old female black Labrador.
Originally been trained and worked as a gundog in Scotland. Jade would be one of the dogs attempting to smell dried-out cancer samples rather than frozen samples – would she find this possible?

Toddy a 5 year old male red coloured mongrel,
The second dog to be trained using dried samples – would the mongrel in the team be up to the task? Toddy was to give us an unpleasant surprise several months later.

Bee, a 6 year old female Cocker Spaniel.
Black and nearly as tiny as Biddy, again from field trial lines.
Cheeky extrovert, naughty but nice, full of her own self-importance. Would Bee be too old a dog to learn new tricks?
and finally -

Tangle, the puppy dog, 6 month old male Cocker Spaniel, chocolate coloured and bred from "hot" field trial champion blood lines. Would the puppy bred to work game adjust to detecting cancer?

What a star he was to become...

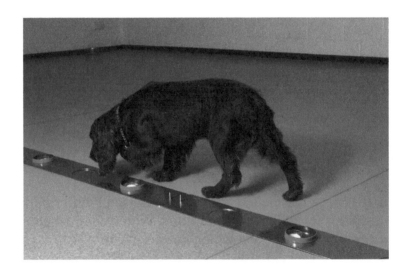

Claire Guest
"Listened to Daisy"

Chapter Thirteen
Some of the dogs trained by Claire Guest

Ruffles

Ruffles was my liver and white English Springer Spaniel and I got him when I was at Swansea University.

Ruffles had never been trained. He was nearly uncontrollable! He would leap on furniture, onto tables scattering everything in all directions. He wouldn't go on the lead, he was a complete handful. If Claire Guest was ever to become a dog trainer here was a supreme challenge to start her on her way!

The university was doing very early work on the effect of dogs on humans and taking dogs into hospitals and rest homes for elderly people. This was many years ago in the very early 1980s and it was pretty much the first time the theory that animals could have a beneficial effect on humans was being talked about seriously.

We were part of the research that suggested that contact and stroking a dog would have a beneficial effect on a person's blood pressure and lower their heart rate. The research at Swansea was headed by Tony Lysons and I did so want to be part of his research team. Tony published two papers that reviewed the effects on a human when we stroke a dog and discovered that the human's heart rate would drop. He also studied the effect on the dog to see if the beneficial effects were mutual, i.e. the dog received similar benefit from being stroked.

At the same time some research was being done by Friedman in Australia and they found that stroking a dog not only lowered the human's heart rate but it also improved the quality of the blood! The effect was to reduce the stress response in dog and human.

With all this early work going on I found it absolutely fascinating. I loved being involved and had been determined to get a dog of my own where I could include first-hand experience. I had no feeling for what type of dog it was but knew there had to be at least one at the rescue centre that would love to come home with me so you can imagine the huge sadness I felt when they assured me that I would never be allowed to own a dog of my own.

But as so often happens in life at that very moment of dark despair lights suddenly shine and someone or something enters your life and turns it around. At this time of my life it was a dog called Ruffles.

Ruffles had not had any training and was all over the place but he had a heart of gold. He was the strongest most loyal and trainable dog you could ever wish for.

It annoys me when people say Springer Spaniels are totally mad, they are only mad because their owners have not done anything to train them! They need stimulation and direction.

I knew I had to train Ruffles and to start with I went to a couple of dog training classes but it all seemed to be about pushing and shoving your dogs to do as you tell them, and standing on leads, and getting them to do simple things. I quickly realised that this dog was far too intelligent for all of that. Why would I want to push his bottom down to get him to sit, or pull and push him around if he could learn what I wanted him to do without any of that.

I started to think about how I had trained Tess – the rat. Tess would push certain buttons when lights come on and for her food and do all the things I asked her without any pushing, shoving, check chains, or forcing. Her training was done by rewarding her every time she got something right. I thought to myself –

'Hang on a sec! If my rat could do it then of course my dog could. He's sitting beside me – looking at me – wanting to know what I want him to do'.

I started to do a lot more training with him based on the techniques I had used with the rat. I used food as a reward but let him make the decision. As soon as he got it right I would respond with *'Oh I like that!'* and give him a reward. He started to make more and more correct decisions each of which was accompanied by me with *'Good dog, I like that'* and a reward of a small piece of food.

It might sound like a very small change from telling your dog what to do and then rewarding it to letting the dog make the decision and then rewarding when it gets it right but it is of huge significance.!

Even with the heel work that caused me the greatest problems with this typically 'mad' springer spaniel wanting to go dashing off here there and everywhere I would stand and wait for him to return, reward and keep eye contact as he walked beside me. He gradually learned that when walking at heel it was all about remaining with the person you were with irrespective of what was going on out there and irrespective of whether there was a lead joined to you.. He knew he could find out all about that when he had his run but when at heel he would keep at my side and keep eye contact.

Traditionally there has been much rubbish talked about eye contact with a dog. For years 'experts' in dog behaviour have stated that the dog makes eye contact because it is trying to dominate you.

It is only in the last 5 years or so that trainers are beginning to acknowledge that some dominant dogs might be trying to dominate you but most are making eye contact to try to say *'Hey, what would you like me to do?'*

Professor Daniel Mills at Lincoln University has published his research that dogs are the only species that look at a human face and analyse our emotional side. The human face is not symmetrical and psychologists recognise that one side of our face reveals a great deal more about our true emotional state than the other. Daniel Mills research showed that dogs concentrate on that side of our face. They are always trying to read our emotions.

If you really love the dog it will show in your face and tell the dog what it needs to know.

I had realised this with Ruffles all those years ago. I used to think to myself *'Hang on- this dog is not trying to dominate me, he's making eye-contact to see what I would like him to do next!'*

Ruffles and I would spend ages just looking at each other. I could clearly see his looking and eagerly saying *'what do you want me to do?'* Within a year I could take him to obedience competitions and win.

In the 1980s training was all about dominating the dog and its responses. I am pleased to say that now in 2014 training has changed and is much more positive. However I sometimes feel the pendulum has swung too far.

Today it all too often becomes all reward and no negative consequences but for a relationship to succeed there has to be mutual respect.

Within the pack, dogs show mutual respect to each other!

The old belief was that there was one dominant dog in each pack effectively controlled all it did whereas in actual fact the control is distributed amongst more than one dog. They will help each other out and there is far more collaboration and coalition between pack members than was originally realised.

That same mutual respect must exist between a dog and owner. The dog must recognise that I respect him as much as he respects me.

That is how you develop the relationship to the next stage. You must engender in the dog that you realise that the dog can do some things a lot better than you and the dog must realise that there are some things you can do better than the dog.

In a dog pack they understand that some dogs are very good at this and some dogs are very good at that. Not all dogs good at everything. Research has now backed all this up.

The mutual respect and ability to read each other's faces and Ruffles' incredibly kind nature led to us being truly soul mates.

I trusted him completely. Everywhere we went we just needed to look at each other to know what the other felt. He became so obedient that at shows people were astounded. *'How on earth did you get him that obedient? I've got a springer and he is totally mad!*

He had a huge amount of energy. We used to walk on the beach at Swansea for hours and he would run for miles. On other occasions when I was on the beach but studying he would stay near me but play tennis ball. He would drop the ball at my feet but if I took no notice he would play a game he invented whereby he would drop it in a gradient and then look away as the ball rolled down the slope, look back and leap after it just as if I had rolled it for him. If there was no slope then he would pat the ball whilst he was looking away look back and again pounce on.

It was quite enlightening to me to watch this dog accept that I had studying to do so couldn't play so he would stay close to me and invent me rolling the ball for him to chase.

The story with Ruffles got very sad.

I finished at Swansea University and was back in Buckinghamshire working at Hearing Dogs when Ruffles started to be really unwell. He was hiding under the bed being continually sick with bloody diarrhoea. He had received a vaccination against Parvovirus but the early vaccinations were less powerful and had clashed with some anti-biotics he was on at the time.

I took him to a vet locally but he was absolutely awful. He put him on painkillers and a small drip but kept saying *'He's not going to pull through, he's definitely not going to pull through'*

I was absolutely devastated by it and couldn't think of anything else. I told Gillian at Hearing Dogs that my dog was dying. *'I think we should have him put to sleep, he's in so much pain'.*

Gillian loved Ruffles *'I think we should make a call first, there is a vet I know who has made a deep study of Parvovirus'*

I phoned him.

'We've learned a lot about Parvo now' came the reply *'if we treat the dog in a certain way we can get them through it. There is a great vet in Aylesbury I know and have worked with and if anyone can get your dog through it he can'*

The vet in Aylesbury phoned me. *'Go and get your dog and bring him to our practice'.*

'What shall I do about his drip?'

'Leave his drip but get him here as quickly as you can'

I went into the vet who had Ruffles but they wouldn't let me see him let alone take him away. The veterinary nurse was saying *'No, no, you can't have him'*

'I want my dog'

'No you can't have him.'

'What do you mean I can't have him? He's my dog'

'You can't have him; he is signed in here for treatment so you can't have him.'

In the end I had to steal my dog.

When he saw me he stood up, wagged his tale and then collapsed unconscious. We wrapped him in a blanket and carried him to my Mum's little green motor. Ruffles was on my knee but was effectively dead.

I carried him into the Aylesbury veterinary practice. The vet we had spoken to appeared straight away, felt for a pulse, shouted to his nurses, they got whatever it was he needed but he looked at me and said *'I think he has gone but I will have a go....'*

By the following morning he'd had a litre and a half of fluid. The vet rang me and said *'I think we are getting somewhere.'*

We were – the vet had saved his life.

The parvo had damaged his intestines and for the rest of his life he had to live on fish and rice and vitamin pills but he was fine. He was so glad to be home.

He recovered well enough to go back to being an outstanding gun dog, obedience dog and a demonstration dog for Hearing Dogs.

He astounded so many people for many could not see how you could train a dog to be perfectly still whilst the guns are firing and to wait to be sent to find the retrieve, and yet the same dog must react on its own initiative and alert a person who is hard of hearing that an event is occurring that needs their attention. These are diametrically opposite commands. The secret is of course that my type of training had few if any commands but relied on the dog's innate intelligence to work out what is required and a quick look at me for confirmation was all that was needed.

In gun dog competitions I would stand next the dog but bend over to take the retrieve from him and make a fuss of him. I was in my 20s at that time and was inevitably competing against men mostly middle aged and many were grizzly but despite my young

age and my dog being relatively unknown my Ruffles would often win the competition hands down.

I remember at a National Game Fair I had decided to wear a lovely pink dress I had bought. I sent Ruffles out on a retrieve and he ran flat out, his spaniel ears flapping and got the fastest time. My fellow competitors were astounded. *'Where did you get that dog from? Who trained it?'.* I wasn't convinced they believed my answers but they were very keen that I send Ruffles on another run to watch him compete. They all gathered behind me and were full of admiration. They asked me to do it again.

'Go again, go again' they all said.

I turned to the crowd of fellow competitors behind me. *'Why on earth would you want me to go again? My dog's already got the best time why do you want me to go again?*

'Never mind that – go again' was the consensus and as I bent over to take his lead and talk to him the quiet voice of one chap near me said *'They like to see you run your dog cause every time you bend over your dog that pretty little dress of yours rides up and you show all your knickers.'*

'Oh No!' crimson red face for Claire – wild guffaws from the massed crowd of men behind me.

I didn't compete with Ruffles in the very top competitions but he went on to win a whole lot of competitions in his lifetime.

Ruffles taught me so much.

It was the first relationship I had with my own dog and I believed then that a combination of prayers and perhaps an angel looking over us had brought him back from death by Parvovirus to a lifetime of happiness for him and for me.

I had almost lost him to parvo when he was 4 years old. He not only survived and became a star at all the gundog competitions we went to but he was still demoing for hearing dogs all over the country when he was 12 years old.

I have a video of him performing but even after all these years I still get overcome with grief at him dying. He lived until 13 and a half years old and I know dogs have a shorter life span than us but he really was a soul mate and an incredibly lovely and loving dog and I missed him terribly once he had died and I still miss him, and I guess I will 'till my dying day.

MINSTREL

As Ruffles was nearing the end of his life I knew I must protect myself from the grief of his inevitable death. I decided to get a liver Flatcoat Retriever. For some reason all through my adult life I seemed to see in my mind's eye the breed and type of dog that was going to be mine.

A Doctor in Devon used to breed flat coat Retrievers and had some liver coloured puppies. I went to Devon to meet them and first saw the Mum and Dad and then the puppies. I really could not pick

out one from the pack as the one I wanted, none really stood out for me.

Eventually I picked out a dog puppy and should have been warned what to expect from him from the off. We were doing all the paperwork when this dog managed to get himself shut in the door, started screaming and hobbling about. I should have known he would constantly wander or even rush headlong into trouble with a smile on his face until he recognised that perhaps he should really be doing something entirely different.

So I came home with this big bundle on my lap and Ruffles is giving me the eye *'What on earth have you got there, and do we want it?'*

I remember when I got them both into the car together. They just sat there eying each other so suspiciously but they actually came to be inseparable.

Minstrel was a total and utter clown!

He was without question the most difficult dog I have ever had to train.

Whereas Ruffles had been manic when he first came home with me and would do 'wall of death' runs around the walls of my student flat in Swansea. Minstrel was so laid back that he could walk into a room of strangers with a body language that would say *'Hi folk, I'm here now so it's time to chill out and relax'.*

I don't know if he was thick. He was certainly bomb proof and would look at me with a quizzical look as if he were trying to fathom something out.

Most dogs are wary of people who look or act a bit odd, but Minstrel would head straight for them, wagging his tail furiously with his body language saying *'Yes! I'm your friend!'* before smothering them with affection. I never saw him afraid of anything in his life, but because he was so affectionate to the unusual being he would get into some terrible fixes.

He was always going off to speak to complete strangers; the stranger they were the better. He was a brilliant gun dog and would be yards ahead of his nearest rival, bringing the retrieve back to me at top speed but if he saw out of the corner of his eye a stranger he would suddenly turn at right angles and hurtle towards them at top speed, scaring them half to death before he had buried them in a multitude of licks and kisses.

How I eventually got him to compete at national level is beyond me and even then if a wandering tramp was passing by I knew we were in trouble. The more unusual the stranger the greater appeal to Minstrel and he just had to embrace them at top speed and with massive enthusiasm.

Ruffles had taught me about communication between a human and a dog but Minstrel taught me how to train the most loveable, naughtiest dog you could wish to own.

His behaviour was idiotic but he was in fact intelligent. He needed his training to be in black and white. *'Yes this is what I want': 'No that is not correct!': 'That is very good',* all the time with consistency and reward when he was correct.

I have trained dogs up to top level in all spheres of life and once they know what is expected of them they are so happy to perform to the best of their ability. With Minstrel we would get to that level of training and understanding when he would decide that he could accomplish the task in a different way and would complete the task in his way and as it suited him. It was no point in telling him off, his attitude was 'am I bovvered?'

Minstrel had no malice in him whatsoever – he just needed to do his own thing in the middle of a brilliant trial. With him I really had to learn how to train a dog. I had to get over to him that in certain situations he has to focus on me and what I want and to do it my way, at other times he can have loads of fun, lark about and do it his way.

Ruffles would watch all this with the air of an older dog amused by the youngster's behaviour and sense of fun. The two dogs were very different in breed, behaviour and instinct but they loved each other.

Minstrel was always messing about and larking around. He was a big Flatcoat Retriever but in fact his coat was always fluffed out and when he went wagging his way to any stranger or different looking individual he would overwhelm them as he tried to lick their faces.

Minstrel reminded me of Rod Hull's 'Emu' in the way he behaved but I eventually managed to come to an understanding of the way to motivate and train a difficult dog. He became a demonstration dog for Hearing Dogs and I used to do a lot of events with him. He was a very good Retriever but very headstrong.

I have become passionate about helping dogs to control and overcome their frustration and I believe that many of the lessons I have learned may apply equally well to people.

Frustration control needs to kick in when animal begins to become excessively frustrated and impulsive. High frustration impedes learning. I spent a long time with Minstrel helping him to control his frustrations and this means that I now work with many dogs who have difficulties in frustration management and cannot control their reactions.

With any young dog I am handling I now always teach them frustration control. In today's world nearly everything is controlled for dog or human. Mum looks after them in the nest, they are fed at regular times.

We often take puppies away from litters before their mother has had the chance to induce frustration control. If they were with mother longer she would teach them that food was not always there on demand. She would push them away however much they might scream they would have to wait until Mum wanted to feed them. She is effectively saying to them *'no sorry, I'm not ready to feed you yet,'* and *'you can scream as much as you like but you won't get any food until you are in control of yourself and quiet'.*

At some point the puppy or child has to learn that there are some things that happen in life that take you right out of that comfort zone and often they cannot change or influence it. At such times they have to control their feelings and frustrations.

The older the dog is when this happens then often the greater is the feelings of frustration at their inability to cope. If a puppy has grown into a full sized and big dog that must now be stopped from jumping up to people the greater frustration it feels at being told off for doing something it has done all its life to date. So far everything has been he or she has wanted now its handlers are changing the rules its lived by to date and it has had no training on how to cope with these changes. It has never had to cope with that emotion before. It has never had to cope with *I can't do that anymore! Why not – I've always done it this way before!*

If it's owners insist then often the dog can't cope with their refusal to let it do something that seemed totally natural to it and was often allowed previously.

'You can't do that!'

'But I want to do it'

'No you can't do it'

In the dog that has never been trained to deal with this emotion it can lead to aggression.

So I teach my puppies that they cannot always have what they want when they want it. One way is to regularly hold a favourite toy that the puppy pulls at and not let the puppy succeed in getting it from you particularly when it is pulling, biting, or bullying. When the puppy effectively says *'Well actually I didn't really want it after all'* then it sits back and gets the toy.

If you teach that to young dogs then they learn that they cannot have everything in life just when they want it. You can't with a puppy go from this point – to that! You have to teach them a bit at a time. Whenever you have a treat in your hand, don't feed it to the puppy that tries to grab it or greedily take it from your hand, wait until it is calm and takes the treat gently.

I often visit people who ask for help. *'I can't cope with this dog, it's a big dog now and it's jumping up all the time, scratching me and growling at me when I try to stop it'*

We have to start with teaching the dog to control its frustrations.

My colleague Kimberley and I have a huge success rate at turning such dogs around to totally acceptable behaviour.

It was Minstrel that started my understanding of a dog's frustration and how by dealing with that you can get even the most difficult dog to the stage when I could use him as a demonstration dog at Hearing Dogs and also as a star retriever.

I had taught him not to jump up at people and also that if he sat and waited he might get treats that he wouldn't get by bullying.

Sadly Minstrel's passion for swimming led to him into an accident that nearly cost him his life. I was walking a footpath alongside a stream and Minstrel had swum under a wide road bridge. I hadn't realised that he had passed through the other side as I was calling him and instead of turning around and swimming back as I was expecting he climbed out of the water and hurtled back straight across the road.

He was hit hard by a car and went bouncing down the road. The car that hit him then drove off, I was running down the road trying to get to him when the next car wizzed up to what it thought was a bin bag but stopped. I got to them. Minstrel looked up at me and wagged his tail but his leg was shattered. We got him into the car and to the vet – the same one that had saved Ruffles. He had two lots of major surgery but it was so good that in later life his leg with the plate in it was stronger than the others.

It just had to happen to Minstrel, he was always bumping into things and people. He was the puppy who got his leg shut in the door whilst I was signing the papers to own him. Now bless him he must recover from a shattering road accident. Recover he did and everyone loved him. He was a clown right up to the day he died. He was the most giving dog. Throughout his lifetime he had no stress in his body whatsoever. I cannot remember a single instance when Minstrel showed any anxiety.

Minstrel never quite got to be a soul mate but we were extremely close and he taught me so much that has stayed with me for the rest of my life and I have used with so many dogs since. Through this knowledge I have been able to save dogs with severe behaviour problems who might otherwise be euthanized . It has taught me to understand that dogs need internal impulsive control.

Minstrel was a great teacher!

Ruffles died when he was 13 and a half years old and indicated that he was ready to leave this life; he was put to sleep in my arms in my Canal Cottage.

Minstrel died when he was just over 13 years old again in my arms.

I had got Dill just before Minstrel died.

Ruffles had been my first dog and I suffered a lot of grief at his going. He and I had shared all the wonders of watching the techniques I had used so successfully on Tess my rat work equally successfully on this wild springer spaniel who was to become a really close friend and soul mate as well as a hugely successful working dog.

Minstrel taught me how to train a really difficult and independent minded dog and I adored him and all his funny and independent ways. To get Minstrel to learn anything was a massive achievement so I learned a great deal from him.

DILL

I bought Dill from a lovely man who used to be a gundog trainer. He was a person that every time you met him he seemed to be a man not in his time. It's an odd observation but the look on his face; his hair; and his manner were almost as though he had gone back in time. This impression was consolidated the first time I visited his home to see the puppies he had. His farm did

everything with rare breeds, shire horses and original farm machinery.

I always had a vision of what my next dog should be and I told him that I wanted a chocolate Cocker.

'I've just had a litter of puppies with a chocolate Cocker in it!'

'Oh I'd be very interesting in seeing it!'

'O.K, come along to the farm'

I did and it was a beautiful sunny day, an old fashioned farmyard, gloucester spotted pigs, chickens climbing all over the old farm machinery, it was a haven.

He bred Cocker Spaniels but instead of breeding the new bloodlines that everyone was talking about in the 1970s that were full of vigour and hard to hold as though they had bred just too much into the dog, he bred the very traditional old-fashioned gun dogs that would walk across fields with you, flush out a rabbit that they would bring back to you. I really liked the way he would talk about his dogs.

Ever since I was a little girl and used to watch 'The Magic Roundabout' on TV I wanted to have a little dog named Dill. I used to sing the show's ditty about him and used to tell people that I am going to get a dog called Dill when I grow up. TV's Dill did lots of aimless running around & retained his love of bones, but with a voice came evidence of a brain (of sorts) and he was sometimes capable of slowing down long enough to engage it, revealing flashes of inspiration and insight along the way

His child-like exuberance usually meant they were rarely fully thought through, which endeared him to many of those watching but he was definitely a "glass half full" kind of dog.

Now was my opportunity to own a real life 'Dill'

The dogs were in kennels and he showed me into them. The Mum came out to greet us. She had a really lovely attitude. Then the pups came out including the chocolate coloured Cocker Spaniel.

I just looked at him and knew immediately that he was my Dill. He was quite shy, but such a wonderful personality that he was subsequently to really enjoy doing everything I asked of him.

I called him out from the kennel and we started playing with a little toy together.

Ruffles' life had ended and he really had been my soul mate. I would trust Ruffles to do anything I ever asked of him. I was able to take him anywhere and he would never let me down. Minstrel was almost the opposite so I was looking for a new dog I could trust 100%.

I was sitting on an old piece of equipment with a small toy, playing with this tiny dog that was looking up at me, fetching the toy to me and connecting. In the car on the way home I sat with Dill on my lap and I knew we were in for a long journey through life together. I wasn't sure where that journey would take us but in the event we were incredibly successful together.

Dill was to take me from being a gundog trainer to winning trials at National Level. He took me through training as a Demonstration Dog for Hearing Dogs, to winning 'Dog Brain of Britain'

I trained Dill to detect Cancer.

By the time we got to set up the tests to prove dogs could sniff cancer Dill was more than 13 years old so I didn't ask him to do the tests and instead trained Tangle but Dill was the first dog to prove to me that he could smell cancer in urine samples.

When we started to get the first cancer samples from hospital via John Church I was training gundogs at high level and I knew that to test dogs to prove they could smell cancer we needed to test through the use of real cancer samples alongside samples from healthy people.

Dill was 12 and a half years old when I heard John on Radio 4 talking about his belief that dogs could smell cancer. A talk that led to Gillian and I phoning the radio station, getting in touch with John, meeting up, running a worldwide symposium and starting to prove our theory's by using our dogs on samples supplied by John.

I needed the samples to really find out if cancer gave off a smell. At this stage Tangle was only 6 months old and I needed to use a dog that I trusted completely Although Dill was getting old at that time I knew that he would tell me if cancer present in the samples gave a different odour.

If a dog could smell cancer then I was confident that I would be able to subsequently train Tangle to detect it but I didn't want to start testing the samples with a dog that had not yet matured to full trust from me.

I needed a dog that I fully trusted and knew would tell me if cancer had a smell.

If Dilly could tell me if there was a difference between the healthy sample and the one from a cancer patient then I could train the younger dog Tangle to a stage that we could put him through the tests that would be needed to prove it.

I started to train Dill by putting metal flower pots on the ground each holding a tea bag one of which one would be Earl Grey tea. I wanted teach him how to find the Earl Grey from each of the others. I would get him to sniff his way along this line of flower pots and to sit and stare at the one that contained the Earl Grey.

O.K. that worked! He learned that pretty quickly so now I was going to get some urine samples from the hospital. I put the samples under the flower pots instead of the tea bags. They were all healthy samples apart from one that was from a cancer patient. I then sent Dill along the line. I used a different – fresh set of samples on each test and within about 10 weeks Dilly was consistently picking out the one that contained the cancer sample.

The sensations we felt as Dill became more and more proficient can be imagined, the hairs stood up on the back of my neck and arms

Claire Guest
"Listened to Daisy"

I knew we were proving something that would have astounding effects on mankind. If dogs could detect cancer by merely sniffing a urine sample look what a fantastic contribution they could make for the early detection of the disease and for simple, inexpensive, unobtrusive inspection of a person's disposition toward cancer on a regular basis.

A urine sample test once a year or more often if cancer is suspected in a person could confirm whether scarce and expensive medical inspection should be employed.

The possibilities were endless but first our results would need to be tested. Dill was getting too old to put through the tests and this is where Tangle came into his own.

Dogs from dog charities, drug sniffers, bomb detecting, and a whole host of other organisations were put through a series of tests in front of a panel of celebrities, veterinaries and dog experts who judged their performance and selected a winner. We handlers were allowed to choose the tests we put our dogs through to show off their skills

I have never met a dog that was as clever as Dill. I used to work him against the top gundog people and they were all in wonder as to how this little dog who could demonstrate answering the phone and alerting deaf owners to events that needed them yet could outperform their specialist gundogs.

In gundog tests the 'retrieve' is thrown a long way behind the dog, or thrown whilst the dog was under cover. The dog is then sent out to find the retrieve and hopefully sets off to the area the kill landed in or quarters the area until it locates it and comes back to its owner at top speed in an attempt to record the fastest time and/or the most sylish performance. Most gundogs towered over little Dill and watchers would often sigh when I came to the mark thinking Dill would not have a chance.

You would hear the shot so you knew the target had been thrown. Dill would stand stock still and cock his head as if listening for the kill to fall to earth. He would then look at me waiting for the eye contact signal that would send him on his way and the judge would often say *'I'm terribly sorry he is so small he never got a chance to see that direction'* He would then instruct me to send my dog away and with no more than a *'Dill fetch'* from me Dill would set off at top speed, exactly straight to the retrieve, return at top speed and inevitably record the fastest time of the day.

One time at a game fair we were competing against one of the top gundog handlers in the country with his top dog, a cocker spaniel twice the size of my little Cocker. The gun fired, the cocker raised his elegant head to see the direction of the retrieve. Dill was too small to see but on the instruction to send your dog - off went Dill like a rocket straight to the kill, picked it up and straight back at top speed to give it to me in my hand. *'Is this what you wanted Mum? Well there you are, here it is!'* as he smiled up at me.

He was so clever and nothing fazed him.

The result would always astound onlookers *'it's like that little dog's got a GPS in it!'* would be a regular response. Dill did this time and time again and nobody worked out how he did it.

To this day I am not exactly sure of the technique he used for he had effectively worked out his own method. Did he use his hearing to detect where it had fallen? Did he use an incredible sense of smell that could pick out the 'retrieve' in mid-air and detect its direction and precisely where it fell to ground? Did he use some other method using senses that are as yet undiscovered in dogs? I have no idea. What I did know was that he had worked out a method that built upon my training to give him incredible success against dogs that seemed far better equipped to beat his times.

I had trained Dill to find articles that people might have lost. If they had dropped their keys somewhere I would get him the scent of the person and send him off to find and back he would come with their missing keys.

We used this skill in the tests we did for 'Dog Brain of Britain'.

Without knowledge of the dog we had set up the scene where someone had lost his keys that were in fact left in the pocket of a jacket that had been put into a washing machine. I had noticed that all the other dogs in the final were extremely well trained but they all worked to their handler's instructions so would do this or that in accordance to instructions given to them. I decided to trust Dilly to work without any instruction from me.

When our turn came I patted my pockets and said *'Oh no Dilly, I've lost my keys, where are my keys?'* and off Dill would go in search.

Dill traced them to the washing machine and then opened the door, climbed inside, got the keys out of the pocket, leapt out of the machine and hurtled back to drop them in my hand. This blew the minds of most people watching and the judges. He then performed all the other tests with similar alacrity.

Dill was declared 'Dog Brain of Britain'.

He was treated like a celebrity and in demand on TV and presentations all over the country. He was even invited to attend Balls and national events. He loved it and I could always trust him to do beautifully whatever I asked.

There was all sorts of TV and film work that resulted and I could take him anywhere in any conditions and he would perform brilliantly and always looked so pleased with himself and for me when each session ended.

Dill taught me that dogs really could work out solutions and to foresee things.

At that time psychologists were telling us that animals did not have the power of deduction they could not foresee a problem and work out a solution. Their cognisant behaviour came about from an accidental discovery that something worked for them rather than from their deduction that it could. It was generally believed that dogs could not sit down and work out a solution to a problem; it could only react to what happens and remember it.

It was confidently thought that only humans had the ability to work out solutions in this way. With Dill you could see him metaphorically sitting down and working out the solution to a

problem. *'If I do that and that and that then this would happen'* then off he would go and solve the problem.

Dill was brilliant, a demonstration dog for Hearing Dogs, winner of numerous gundog events, winner of 'Dog Brain of Britain', starred in many TV shows and films, and was a real celebrity. He also put me on the map as an outstanding dog trainer.

When he died he left a great big hole in my life that could not be fully filled.

Woody was a son of Dill and though Dill never successfully threw himself in his puppies Woody filled my life with a whole new chapter of events and love. But Dill will never be forgotten – his portrait sits over my fireplace and we smile at each other each and every day.

TANGLE

Tangle was always an old soul even at 6 months old when I started training him to sniff out cancer.

Dill had proved that a dog could distinguish the smell of cancer and indicate which sample contained it by sitting in front of the cancerous sample and staring at it.

Dill was by then an old dog so Tangle was trained to take over the detection for all the trials that would be necessary to show that a dog could succeed.

Tangle's approach to life has always been phlegmatic but he took his work extremely seriously and was enormously successful. He had a steady methodical way of working, never becoming over-excited or over-awed no matter how many cameras or reporters were crowding him as he worked.

As Dill aged then Tangle took over as major detection dog and became the face of the charity. The press featured 'Tangle – the Cancer Detection Dog' and his picture went around the world. His record as the most successful detection dog in the BMJ publication gave us great publicity and hope for the future.

He was very efficient at everything I asked him to do. He has demonstrated cancer detection in very many locations and has always put in a first class performance with tremendous accuracy always looked undemonstrative but conscientious.

When the BMJ article came out Tangle was demonstrating up to 10 times a day with great accuracy and never any fuss.

My relationship with Tangle differed from that from Ruffles and Dill because he was always self-contained and never demanded any additional attention. He is now a 12 year old and an old man greatly loved and will leave a huge hole in my life when he finally goes.

Dill had a long and enormously happy life and died of old age. As we write this book Tangle is still with us leading a life of retirement. When a new study was started I knew that I needed another dog to train to detect cancer. Here was another of my strange visions kicked in and I knew I needed a fox red Labrador however rare they were and difficult to find. She would be called Daisy.

DAISY

By now in my life I had loads of gundog friends but none knew of a fox red Labrador puppy for sale. I was looking in The Shooting Times, not because I am a fan of shooting animals or birds but because the results of gundog trials

were reported in it. There was an advert for a Labrador for field trials and peg work.

I was looking for a gundog with the calmness and patience of a pegdog and the intelligence and responsiveness of a field trial competitive dog.

I didn't know the person who had advertised but made a phone call whilst thinking I was probably making a mistake as it would be a gundog breeder trying to get me to buy a dog that was unsuitable for the tasks I had planned for it.

However it was a lady who answered the phone and I said *'This might sound strange but I train gundogs. I also trained the dog that smells out cancer that has just been reported in the British Medical Journal. I am looking for a dog that I can train up to continue that task.'*

She gave the impression that she thought I was some sort of mad woman phoning her. *'Sorry, you are doing what?'*

'I train gundogs and I trained the dog to sniff out cancer that has just been reported in the British Medical Journal and I'm looking for a fox red Lab, dog or bitch!'

'Oh! I've got three fox reds in this litter but they have all been taken but there is a small question mark over one of them, I don't know if the person is going to have it or not'.

'Oh right! Well I have a strong feeling about what I want so maybe the puppies might not fit my plans, but I would love to meet them.'

We talked for a while longer and she said *'Why don't you come down and meet the puppies?*

I got exactly the same feeling as I had years before when I went down to meet the litter that contained Dill. I am never sure if it is the way the light reflects, or the way the sun is shining at that moment or some other reason but I know at that moment fate is taking a hand.

So I went down to the farmyard that was at the back of this beautiful old manor house in Kent. The lady, now a wonderful friend, answered the door

'Come in, the puppies are in the kitchen.'

It was a glorious old kitchen with an Aga and chaos everywhere. Mum, a black Labrador comes out wagging her tail at me, and there were the six puppies, I felt sure my 'Daisy' was here.

'You can look at this puppy, or this puppy, or this one'

One of them was a fox red, a little aloof but exactly what I was looking for.

'Which would you like?'

'I did say I was looking for a fox red but you said they were already spoken for.'

'Ah well that is not exactly true, it is that this one is a very special puppy and I have been waiting for a special owner. I think you might be her!'

171

There was no doubt the puppy she was talking about exactly matched my vision of 'Daisy'

Daisy was mine and came home with me to start an incredible life together.

I kept in touch with Biddy the breeder and kept her up to date with all Daisy was achieving. I am not sure she believed all my missives until Daisy started to appear on television demonstrating her cancer detection. I would always send her a message *Watch so-and-so show on TV tonight – Daisy is appearing'*

Many years later I was to discover that she was great friends with Betsy Duncan-Smith who was to become a Trustee in the charity Medical Detection Dogs we were to subsequently form. Betsy is a wonderful kind lady who gives us tremendous encouragement and support and it later turned out that she had known Biddy (Bridget Wood - the breeder of Daisy) for many years.

Biddy is a nationally renowned artist who has painted portraits of animals including those belonging to the Royal Family. She painted a picture of Daisy that is quite stunning. She has somehow captured Daisy's soul on a painting.

Right from the start of her life Daisy had a temperament and attitude of a grown-up friend. She was always calm and obedient, biddable and learned things almost immediately. Unlike Minstrel who had preceded her - Daisy was rarely in trouble. She was just a really good puppy. I struggle to remember anything she has ever done wrong.

Dill had proved to my satisfaction that a dog could sniff out cancer and the potential of this ability was now getting incredibly important in my mind.

I thus started training Daisy to identify cancer samples from the time she came home with me at 12 weeks old. I wanted to find out if a puppy could succeed and identify cancer in various samples but also needed to define whether a dog trained from puppyhood gained greater accuracy than a dog that started training at a later date.

Daisy now has an incredible success rate measured at 93% accuracy at detecting cancer samples from others but is that due to her incredibly lovely temperament or to the early training. At the time this book is being written we just don't know - the jury is still out..

From 12 weeks old I would get the cancer sample out and let her sniff it before I fed her. Then I started to hide it in her bed and get her to find it. As soon as she found it I would give her a click and a treat. So very early on she learned that this cancer sample was incredibly important.

A little later on in her life I made it a little harder for her by having two pots, one was a cancer sample the other was clear. When she correctly identified the yes sample she got her click and treat and she learned it very quickly. Tangle was my main demo dog but Daisy was progressing very well. I have her nephew starting training with us as this book is being written and we are starting him in the same way so it will be very interesting to see if he achieves the incredible accuracy of Daisy.

Daisy has always been very close to me. She sleeps on my bed, she walks alongside me wherever I go - we share a life.

Daisy has always been excellent at cancer detection and particularly bladder and prostate cancer.

Daisy's 93% accuracy should be measured alongside some of the medical tests for similar cancers that can measure only 25% accuracy before invasive medical examination is needed. Even after this painful examination one in three medical results will be incorrect.

There are occasions when medical tests for a particular type of cancer can give a patient an all-clear only for them to subsequently be diagnosed with a different kind of cancer that the medical test had not covered.

Daisy's nose detects cancer in a sample so cancers other that the one that might be suspected are discovered.

We have had our Ethics proposal accepted by Bucks NHS Trust's fantastic team of clinicians. This is an intensive but understandable examination of the way we will handle cancer samples and the data we glean from them as well as protecting the identity of the cancer patient. Our charity Medical Detection Dogs is thus cleared to start training a new batch of dogs

This exciting move forward means we are now able to make a start examining if our doge can detect Breast Cancer from breath tubes. The patient breathes into a tube that is then sealed and tested by our dogs to see if cancer is present.

This is just the 'Proof of Principle' we need to prove the link through rigorous testing that dogs can detect Breast Cancer through the breath of a patient. We will train the dogs on 'known' cancer samples (YES/NO) and then on unknown samples.

We have some of the top specialist helping us with the trials and we will be jointly publishing a paper on the results.

The potential savings of patient's lives and costs to the National Health Budget if we can prove that dogs can accurately diagnose breast cancer from a breath tube is huge. Regular testing at very low cost becomes possible so that early detection can result in early treatment if our dog's diagnosis is positive giving much better chance of patient survival. Equally hugely expensive NHS equipment, personnel and specialists are saved from much of the diagnostic work and can concentrate on the actual treatment of patient that we would know have cancer.

For almost the first time since we started trying to prove that dogs could sniff out cancer we can begin to talk about the potential ways the dogs can impact upon humans and the methods of diagnosis.

In all our early years I was shunted into the side-lines as a curiosity, often left to feel that the 'experts' and those in authority saw me as the mad woman with dogs rather than take the trouble to look methods and the results we were achieving.

This began to change for me when we took two of our dogs to Milan to do a demonstration to the city dignitaries and medical experts. I had never had first-hand experience of the paparazzi before but as we arrived at the location we were to conduct the demonstration we were surrounded by flashing TV and cameras photographing us and all the dignitaries and celebrities.

This was to be the first ever demonstration of Cancer Detection dogs in Italy and all the media were reporting, photographing and filming. I just was not expecting such a vast coverage.

We were to perform the demonstration on a stage with a massed audience watching. I was nervous as to how the dogs would perform in front of such a forbidding crowd. Nearly all our previous tests and demonstrations had been conducted to much smaller audiences and for just a few press or TV cameras.

We set up the samples and stepped out on stage to give a short presentation of our work and then brought on Lucy – the other dog we were using. Rob went out with her and bedlam started, cameras were flashing, paparazzi were all jostling for position and trying to get the dog's attention for their photograph. It was chaos, you couldn't see a thing because of all the flashes from the cameras, and they were going non-stop. The crowd were all moving about and pushing each other to get a better angle for their photo. They were all within 8 feet of us and poor Lucy's attention was taken completely away from the job she had come to do and though by no means a shy dog it was all too much for her and she backed away from unaccustomed 'madness' of the group in front of her and away from the samples.

The crowd were reminded that the dogs had come to do a job so please don't crowd or distract her by trying to get her attention. With this type of reception was our entire journey going to be a waste of time, effort and reputation?

A deep breath and bring on Daisy. Her beautiful eyes took in the crowd in front of her. She paused just long enough to take the whole scene in and then she managed to shut them all out of her mind as she started on the job she had been trained to do.

As soon as she saw the samples go down she looked at them then looked at me and it was one of those occasions that is unique to those who have developed a close rapport with their dogs. At that moment there was complete trust between Daisy and me and she knew what I was expecting from her. At such moments the rest of the world disappears and you are doing something that you do together completely for each other.

Daisy was perfect!

Everyone in the audience was completely amazed.

Those unique moments between you and your dog are magical and almost mystical as they go deeply into both your psyches and emotions.

My relationships with Daisy, Dill, and Ruffles have always been blessed with such moments.

Despite all the work I did on Skinnerbox at Swansea University and the studies in the intervening 30 years, the conclusive evidence of 'Theory of Mind' in dogs seems exclusive though most involved believe it to be true.

I have a lifetime experience of such innate ability of dogs yet many people still doubt their ability to look at a problem and work out a solution.

With no conclusive evidence of whether or not dogs are simply responding through 'trial and error' as the behaviourists such as Skinner would describe or have the 'Theory of Mind'. It fascinates me because of its implications at Medical Detection Dogs.

We are obtaining outstanding results on both in cancer detection and the medical assistance partnerships where, as this book is being written, we have nearly 50 dogs living with and improving the lives of those who have life threatening diseases.

Is there a great deal more we could achieve with the dogs if we understood how their minds and their souls really worked?

When you look at the accuracy and success Daisy had in Milan and continues to achieve with her work under all kinds of audiences and circumstances including the demonstration at one of the Royal Palaces to Prince Charles, Camilla Duchess of Cornwall, and invited guests and to all kinds of medical, political and social audiences, all done with the wonderful eye contact before she starts, is it any wonder that I believe there is still lots to learn about a dog's ability and relationship with humans?

Our training has proved that the traditional ways of training a dog are not necessarily correct.

Traditional methods dominate the dog and effectively use bullying to get the dog to do what you want. I was 14 years old when Barbara Woodhouse was at the height of her powers with her TV shows but even then I was convinced that her methods were wrong. She was dominating the dogs instead of sharing the intelligence of the dog and owner. I would cry out to the television *'No, that's wrong! That's not the way to train a dog!'* but hey what did I know?

Yet interesting enough those same instincts I had as a 14 year old are the ones that are bringing us such incredibly successful results with the dogs trained by Medical Detection Dogs.

Traditional teaching was to dominate the dog, don't look it in the eye, or if you do you must stare it out to dominate it. Don't smile at your dog else it will feel you are baring your teeth and so on.

It is all such nonsense!!!

I love the work done by Professor Daniel Mills that has been published over the last 5 years. He has proved that dogs study the human face to read the mood of the human to know how to react to them and what they expect of their dog.

Of course you must look your dog in the eye - how else do you make eye contact that welds the thoughts of owner and dog.

Of course you must smile at your dog. If the dog sees you are happy the dog will be happy.

Claire Guest
"Listened to Daisy"

I have been asked many times for the secrets of our training and following this publication Terry and I will be working on a book yet to be titled but along the lines of *'How to train your dog – the Claire Guest way'*

Meantime we are producing a book of the charity – Medical Detection Dogs. It has reached a stage when as soon as I start talking about it to any audience or individual I realise how incredibly exciting it is.

The other day we had a visit at the charity from a 30 year old man who was suffering so many hypos and being given emergency 'glucogen' injections by his wife 3 or 4 times a day. He broke down in tears when telling us about it, feeling his active life was over.

When you think how simple it is for us to match him with one of our medical assistance dogs who will predict his attacks and get the blood testing kit and sugar to prevent them, you realise we can help give him his life back.

We have more than 50 dogs currently out with clients dramatically improving their life styles as well as introducing them to an incredible fellowship with an animal that is helping them to live a fuller life.

Just think of the work being performed daily by these medical assistance dogs and the tremendous difference our cancer detection dogs can make you will realise just how much good we can do.

I was a young girl and when I kept getting thrown as I tried to mount my first ever pony I remember my Grandmother saying to me *'Claire. Always remember wherever you are and whatever you are doing your Guardian Angel is there to help you,*

When I think about the way incredible people appeared in my life story just when I needed their help and skills and of the way my dogs and horses have communicated with me, even to Daisy warning me of a deep cancer in my chest in time for it to be treated and leaving me fit to continue the development and work of the charity, I really do understand my 'Nanna's' words.

Claire Guest
"Listened to Daisy"

Chapter Fourteen
Proving Dogs CAN sniff cancer
and other life threatening diseases!

The Charity Medical Detection Dogs was originally set up with the name Cancer and Bio-detection Dogs and though the following article was written in 2008 and much of the work and methods have been updated since then, we thought it would provide an interesting background to our charity for our readers.

Claire Guest
"Listened to Daisy"

Cancer and Bio-detection|**Dogs**

We work with researchers from the charity Amerderm, which is part of the Buckinghamshire NHS Trust. Our work seeks to establish the extent to which the olfactory ability of dogs and other animals can be used to diagnose cancer and other diseases in humans.

The first study, entitled 'Canine Olfactory Detection of Human Bladder Cancer a Proof of Principle', was published in the British Medical Journal September 2004. This was the first scientifically robust study to support anecdotal reports that dogs may be able to identify the odour of cancer. A retired orthopaedic surgeon, Dr John Church, initiated this work at the end of 2002. His interest arose from an anecdotal story published in the Lancet in 1989, which described a woman whose pet dog showed a persistent interest in a mole on her leg. This proved to be a malignant melanoma, the most serious form of skin cancer. Cancers being identified by dogs have not been restricted to skin cancer, but also include cancer of the bowel, cervix, and breast.

The notion that dogs can smell cancer is not far-fetched. Over the centuries, physicians have been aware that many diseases have a characteristic odour. Dogs are renowned for their sense of smell. Some estimates put a dog's sense of smell up to 100,000 times more sensitive

than ours. For centuries man has made use of the scenting abilities of dogs to track people and more recently, to detect drugs and explosives. Cancer cells are known to produce chemical compounds that differ from those made by normal cells. It is therefore not unreasonable to think that some may have distinctive odours. We intend to use the olfactory capabilities of our dogs to identify these odours.

Claire Guest
"Listened to Daisy"

It is anticipated, in the long-term, that these findings will lead to the production of an electronic nose machine that GPs can use in surgeries. We believe from the current information we have that this may well be a possibility. We have had discussions with scientists who have shown strong interest in the production of an electronic nose if we can provide the necessary scientific information. We first need to establish a number of things: what odour signature the dogs are using to detect the presence of cancer, to what extent, if any, the dogs can distinguish between various types of cancers, and to what degree of accuracy the dogs can indicate the presence of different cancers. In addition we will need to discover what samples from the body a dog can use to reliably identify the presence of a particular cancer, and whether a dog can use these to reliably detect the internal 'invisible cancers'.

Our current research with Amerderm seeks to investigate some of the above. However there is considerably more work to be done. Our findings could lead to major advances in the understanding and diagnosis of cancer. Our intention is to raise sufficient funding to fully examine the potential in this field. In order to more fully examine this potential, we would like to be able to fund substantially more clinical research doctor time, to act at the interface between patients in Buckinghamshire Hospitals Trust and our cancer research.

In addition to the above cancer research, in accordance with our overall objects, we also train and provide medical Assistance Dogs. The majority of these hypo-alert dogs are trained to assist unstable type 1 diabetics with poor hypoglycaemic awareness. The dogs are trained to identify and alert their owners to low blood sugar levels, and so prevent an imminent hypoglycaemic episode. These dogs greatly improve safety and quality of life for these clients.

Claire Guest MSc CEO and Director of Operations.

Useful references and Information Regarding Canine Olfactory Detection.
www.amerdermtrust.co.uk; British Medical Journal , September 2004: Olfactory detection of human bladder cancer by dogs: proof of principle study. Willis, Church, GUEST et al

In 2004 when we had completed the first round of tests which proved that dogs could sniff out cancer we were hoping to get it published in a prestigious medical journal. We decided to submit a paper to the BMJ (British Medical Journal) – arguably the most prestigious medical journal in the UK. We were all terrifically excited by the prospect. When we got the news that our paper had been accepted we knew this was a huge step forward.

At that stage our group included me, Carolyn Willis – the lead author from the Bucks NHS Trust, John Church and his family.

My husband was still a part of the team but he always gave the impression of never believing we would prove that it could be done or that we could develop the results into a full blown charity defining the way dogs may be used for medical assistance. The acrimonious and terrifying way he left me ended his connection with the project.

As soon as our paper was published all hell was let loose, press arrived from all over the world, media cameras were arriving daily, Sky brought along a lorry with a huge satellite dish on board so that they could transmit directly from our site.

I was still at Hearing Dogs and they allowed us to film from their centre. I had trained the dogs in my spare time and the ones we used had all belonged to me. Invites came in to appear on Breakfast Television and on numerous chat shows so suddenly people were talking about dogs that can smell cancer.

However there was an immediate wave of scepticism from the big cancer institutions. They decried the advent of dogs sniffing cancer. They ridiculed the size of the sample used in testing and the results. They countered the positive response we were getting in the media with the message *'Don't let us get excited about this. The tests have not been done on a big enough sample and the Cambridge University tests trying to do the same thing had returned negative results. Also bear in mind the impracticality of having a dog in every health centre.'*

We were very upset! For one thing had never envisioned that there should be a dog in every medical centre! We felt that there was scope to have a number of Medical Detection Dogs units around the country to which medical centres could send urine, or even breath samples to give the opportunity of early assessment of the possibilities of cancer in their patients.

To make matters worse the organisations producing such negative reactions to the news had made no effort to come along and see what we were doing or to test our results. They didn't even reply to the many invitations we gave them.

There was a wave of scepticism from most of the 'experts' in the field of cancer research and in the media.

'Oh it can't be done

We've heard these rumours before but nothing has come of them'

They are just using anecdotal evidence but there is no proof.

The Cambridge trials proved that dogs couldn't sniff cancer so why are these people saying they can?

Don't get excited – it will never happen!

The widespread scepticism knocked my confidence.

Had we overlooked something?

Were our positive results just a matter of luck?

Why it was that almost nobody believed our results?

With my spirits deflated I rechecked our methods and all our results and despite all the adverse responses I became determined that we were correct. Dogs could and did smell cancer!

The thing that stayed in my mind was the failure of the sceptics to actually visit us and check our methods and results.

In the midst of the chaos caused by our excitement at getting our message out to the world followed by the almost complete refusal of the 'experts' to countenance our results it was easy to overlook that most cancer specialists had spent 5 years or more getting their medical qualification and perhaps another 5 years or more becoming cancer specialists. It cannot have been easy for them to accept that a dog can be trained in 3 or 4 months to sniff out cancer, let alone the possibility that the dog may be more accurate than they at doing so.

Carolyn was doing the interviews on our behalf and at every interview she would stress how important all our work could be for the future of the NHS. Sadly following every interview Cancer

UK would field interviewees decrying the results. Their dismissive response to us was causing many of the medical professionals who had an open mind and wished to find out more to keep their heads down until more facts could be found to support the findings of the 'mad woman with dogs claiming that they sniff out cancer' (an image I seemed to be generating amongst those decrying our work).

At that time I just couldn't see how we were going to get through this mountain of scepticism. Other doubts came to my mind. Was our trial too small to prove conclusively that our dogs were sniffing out cancer?

Could we have missed some significant point in our tests that distorted our results?

How on earth were we to progress from here?

An important factor about training dogs to sniff out cancer is that you need excellent samples from cancer patients that can be placed with healthy samples from other people of the same profile – age, sex, body weight, symptom matched controls etc. Without them our research and training was at an end. With all this scepticism from the Cancer organisations where could I get the samples we needed?

A programme on Channel 4 had followed the tests set up under the auspices of Cambridge University where the tests seem to prove that dogs could NOT smell cancer. None of their dogs were successful. I was quite confident I knew why they had been unsuccessful whilst we had succeeded.

It bears back to the reference made earlier about a Monet painting.

When training dogs you need to make it aware of the precise thing it is looking for in the picture (I usually quote the simile of looking for a red flower in a Monet). You need to have a lot of pictures (samples) so that the dog defines the 'painting that has the red flower' but ignores other scents that are coming to it from that sample. To continue with the simile - if you use too few then it might be that the samples you use have a tree as well as a red flower and the dog will give a positive answer whenever a tree is present especially if your reward system has not gone on to only reward when there is a red flower and no tree or other distracting object.

This simile is good for I believe that a dog's nose defines a whole fog of scents in every human sample and needs to isolate the actual cancer smell from all those that surround it and not sit and stare at the sample (the indicator that it is cancerous) just because it has the smells of the items that surrounded the cancer in the training samples.

Over use of samples in training teaches the dog to 'memorise' the packet – 'this one was a NO'; 'this one was a YES'; leading it to just look at the complete 'Monet' and remembering the frame!

Many dog trainers set the dog a task and reward it when successful but I try to go one stage further and train dogs to be problem solvers. To do that you need a multitude of samples each containing other scents until the dog has learned that the task was to sit and stare only when that one particular scent is present.

The samples we had been getting from the cancer wards defined their content and I would spend hours sorting them to be a sequence that the dog could follow that would gradually and steadily allow it to wean out the surrounding smells and just seek the one that indicated cancer was present.

With the tests completed and our paper proving our case published in the most prestigious medical journal in the UK we thought that money would roll in to support our work and take it further toward setting up a valid organisation that could give invaluable help to the National Health Service and to those who might have cancer. Unfortunately no such thing occurred.

The usual result we got when seeking funds was *'It was all very interesting but we cannot see the relevance. It was a very good test but now it's over – that's it!'*

'No that isn't it! I would plead. *'Now we have proved that dogs can detect cancer what else can they detect? We used urine samples but*

can dogs smell diseases on a person's breath? Can they give early warning of oncoming diseases?'

I could see in the eyes of the listeners that the concepts I was discussing were outside their capacity to accept and it was really depressing. I really felt I was banging my head against a brick wall.

We published our report in 2004 and after 12 months of trying I was beginning to think it was all going nowhere. I felt like my vision was being taken away. The constant rejection was causing me to question the concept I had of Medical Detection Dogs. I almost started to believe the non-believers.

John Church and my Dad still retained their passion for the whole project and they along with the leaders of some other assistance dogs charities urged me not to give up and between them all they kept me going.

Sensible people saying to me *'Now, now don't be put off, it is a great project and we are right behind you'* encouraged me to take up the reins and try even harder to raise the funds and secure the samples that would allow us to continue.

I went back to Carolyn Willis (Bucks NHS Trust) and she was keen to do a second study looking at whether dogs could continue to succeed over a much bigger sample size. She managed to get approval and we jointly financed the second study. The finance covered the first part of the study and though we finished up financing the end of the study ourselves the start-up was enough to recharge our batteries and determination to prove once and for all that dogs could, or could not, smell cancer.

By 2006 with the second study underway it was time to leave Hearing Dogs. This meant that I would be training the dogs in my parent's kitchen but with no longer earning a salary and my marriage in a very precarious state it was a safer option.

My sister Simone had two young children and time at home when they were at school so she used to prepare and set out all the samples for me. For the second study we made extensive use of cameras so that the recording of the dog's performance could be more accurately observed and displayed.

In 2006 we had become determined to set up a charity using dogs for Medical Assistance and through 2006 and 2007 my Dad conducted all the research that was necessary as well as all the negotiations and discussions with the Charities Commission.

We had found a location in a near derelict office at Westcott in 2007 where the second test was completed in 2009 but not published until 2011. It was freezing cold at Westcott and all our funding was going on the testing and training. Often we were so poor that we just did not have enough money to pay the cost of heating and it needed to be switched off for days at a time. I had a few volunteers working with me and my despair at returning to these freezing, leaking premises after radiotherapy to 'zap' my breast cancer was alleviated by the bravery of those helpers wrapped in a multitude of clothing and often blue with the cold as they worked in the freezing conditions.

A journalist Richard from the Bucks Herald visited us at Westcott; liked what we were trying to do; and became determined to do all he could to bring us publicity and plead for anyone with practical skills to spend some time with us helping to improve the appalling conditions we worked under.

In response to his article people kept arriving to help. They painted the woodwork, mended all the things that were broken, helped to put up shelving and dividing areas and generally make life much more comfortable for all of us.

He offered to do an article supporting any major fund-raising we might do but with only a few helpers we felt restricted as to the choice of events we could organise. In the end we thought of a parachute jump and Richard said he would join us on it.

Richard, Simone, and Rob Harris (the trainer who had started with us full time), and I, took off into the skies to float down to earth on individual parachutes. Thankfully none of us were injured and the publicity raised by Richard's article in the Bucks Herald resulted in the inward trickle of much needed donations and funding. We had managed to get a lot of sponsors for our jump and it raised about two and a half thousand pounds which at that stage of our charities development was a huge amount of money.

A gentleman who was a huge supporter introduced us to the 'County Set' and we began to get spoken about at functions that also helped the inward trickle of donations and funds.

The Sheriff of a county in England is a high honorary position awarded to an incumbent for a year and they attend many of the top functions in the county. With his support acceptance of our charity was growing rapidly, particularly in our own county but sadly the medics were still sceptics despite all our efforts to reassure them that our goal was to use the work of our dogs to provide information to assist them and sit alongside theirs and in no way to replace them.

Cancer UK were completely implacable. I invited them to all our presentations, open days and to individual visits but they would not come, they wouldn't even reply to my invites or and contact we tried to make with them. Years later they have attended a demonstration at the centre and we are in correspondence with a number of supportive researchers. This is another significant breakthrough.

Thankfully every now and again someone would come through and want to see what we could do. Professor Karol Sikora a very eminent oncologist from Imperial College was one such. He spent time with us and watched the dogs working and thought they were brilliant. He was sure that this should be driven forward. He became very supportive and would come to as many of our functions as he could.

Just to have his name amongst those present was giving us tremendous credibility and he allowed us to use his name whenever it would help. It all made a huge difference to us and to our confidence that we were on the correct and very worthwhile path.

He was marvellous and our major breakthrough in terms of a real cancer professional giving his name to all we were doing. The Chairman of The Bucks NHS Trust became very supportive and we were realising that if we can get people through our door, where they could actually see the dogs working and the science of our research, they would usually become convinced that there could be a very exciting future for this unique form of detection of disease through odour recognition.

Throughout 2009 we were still training dogs to sniff out cancer but had also trained our first two dogs for Medical Assistance by alerting owners to oncoming hypos (low blood sugars) in Diabetes.

That was a turning point for the charity.

At that point in time I had come to believe that dogs could smell all diseases in humans. I had come to the conclusion that disease caused a biochemical change in the human body and the dog's incredible sense of smell could detect it.

Some of the Trustees were concerned that we did not in the early

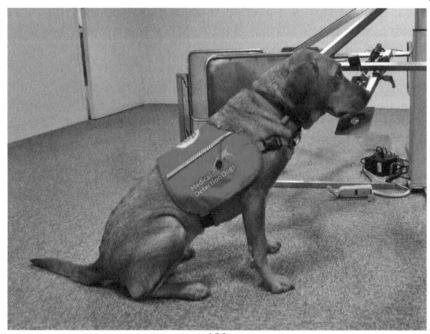

years spread our research too wide and lose our focus on cancer. I could understand their concerns but I always believed that the medical assistance side could support our work on cancer detection.

My observations confirmed that the assistance programme would be much more acceptable to financial supporters and raise a great deal more funds in the early days of our charity than our work in detecting cancer simply because the assistance dog 'model' is already fully accepted. Guide dogs are well recognised.

People were much more comfortable with the training and support of dogs to live with people and warn of oncoming attacks of diabetes or other life threatening diseases than they were of dogs at a centre 'sniffing' out Cancer. In their eyes Medical Assistance Dogs were put on a par with other Assistance Dogs such as guide dogs, hearing, dogs, dogs for the disabled and so on so they would be readily accepted as worthy of support, but 'Cancer Sniffing' – this was a whole new threshold for them to cross.

I was always sure we needed to keep both sides of the charity together. We needed to keep on pushing the concept of Medical Assistance Dogs be they living with the owners and detecting oncoming life threatening events or working from a centre giving early detection of cancer and other life threating diseases.

One side would support the other. Both sides would help gain the acceptance of what dogs can do to help the medical profession.

When I put in an application for sponsorship of 3 dogs to train as Cancer Sniffing dogs we would often be turned down.

If I put in an application for 3 Medical Assistance Dogs to live with and help their owners by early detection of oncoming attacks it would usually be granted with very little questioning.

Assisting our application was the common knowledge that diabetes high blood sugar has an odour that the human can smell, so it was conceivable that a dog could signal it in advance. 'Ketones' only occurs at one end of the scale but the fact that humans had smelt an odour similar to pear drops on the breath of people with diabetes helped the credibility of Assistance Dogs.

I resolved to raise money for Assistance Dogs would be spent on their programme and money in our general funds would support the Cancer detection dogs.

By 2010 we had changed the name of the charity from Bio-detection Dogs we thought was confusing people as to our purpose. It took us some time to find the correct name but we finally settled for Medical Detection Dogs.

We were then confident that we could afford to move away from our location at Westcott into something more in keeping with what we were trying to do and found the ideal premises at Great Horwood – just outside Aylesbury in Buckinghamshire.

We moved on a freezing cold day by borrowing a horse box driven by a volunteer 'Maria', loading it with all our equipment and towing it through the snow to Great Horwood.

Then Kimberley joined us. I had felt that what I needed was a very good dog trainer who trained in the way I believed in. Preferably a person who suffered from diabetes as I had no practical knowledge of the disease. At a talk I was giving a bubbly girl attended that Rob knew to be a good dog trainer and had invited.

She was keen to join us so I talked to her about dogs and I could see she shared many of the same ideals and concepts as I did. As we explored further she said *'Actually I am a Type 1 Diabetic'*

There was no doubt in my mind - *'You've got the job!'*

We trained a dog for her and her first-hand knowledge of the condition and of working the dog proved to be a great asset as we continued to train dogs to give early warning of an oncoming attack.

She has her own business with dogs with behavioural problems. She often gets called in to see dogs who seem to be beyond redemption and are scheduled to be put down and sometimes calls me in to assist. We have an incredible success rate for turning those dogs around with something approaching an 87%

success rate at curing them of their problems. This is always satisfying and enables me to 'give back to the dogs'.

I trust Kimberley's judgement completely and as we have expanded I would have been lost without the ability to delegate a great swathe of my work to her. Similarly I am blessed with Simone working alongside me. Simone's real speciality is working with partnerships of owner and dog she has a fantastic ability to get that right and to help the owner to understand what the dog is telling them and what it needs.

The people I needed have arrived and I am so pleased we pursued the path we did for the assistance dogs did indeed keep us afloat until now – 2014 when the cancer dogs are coming into their own.

At long last we are beginning to get acceptance from the medical profession or at least from some highly influential sections of it.

I knew I needed to do some greater research on the ability of dogs. I spoke to one of our sponsors – a huge European Food Company. Our contact there was a lovely guy who was very passionate about his company's food. He really does believe in its nutritional value and quality. He was very interested in working dogs and whether the food they were fed would affect their performance. Their animal feeds are sold all around the world. We were intent on researching the capability of dogs to establish just how powerful their sense of smell was. It would be easy to expand that research to establish how diet might affect the performance of a dog.

At that time there was much anecdotal evidence on the power of a dog's sense of smell. and literature reported a huge variation of value on the dog's nose.

- Did it have 10 times the capacity of a human nose?
- 100 times?
- 1,000 times?
- Or even a million times?

All these values were being claimed but nobody really knew.

We were the right people to do this research and that our working environment using the carousel was the right place to conduct the tests.

We were lucky to obtain the sponsorship for us to complete the tests. It was the biggest money we had received into the charity up to that time. We used 10 dogs.

The first thing we discovered was that when a dog has reached its lowest threshold if we keep it there then after a couple of weeks it produces even better results. We began to realise that the dog's nose was reacting a bit like the body of a human athlete. The athlete can run or jump and get a good result but if you keep them training for a few weeks their performance improves, so it was with the dogs. Also, if they had a rest from the tests for a few weeks and then came back to it their performance would have deteriorated but within the next few weeks of training it would come back up to the performance they were achieving before the rest break. This is again very similar to the human athlete – stop running for a few weeks and it takes another couple of weeks to get back to best performance.

Such results were also proving our training and testing to be accurate. The dogs were not just guessing they were reacting exactly correctly when confronted with the one sample on the carousel that contained the part we had trained them to look for.

I was very keen to find out just how low we can record a dog succeeding in detecting a smell. Once again was it one part in 10; one part in 100; 1,000; 1,000,000 or one part in an even greater sized sample? We had our own theories but nobody really knew.

We tested but had to give up these tests when the samples got to be one part in 1,000,000,000,000!

We had to give up because the scientists who were setting up the samples and reviewing the tests could not produce samples greater than one part in a Trillion!

This helped us in a huge acceptance of our work. Interestingly it did not depend on the type of dog necessarily as we used different breeds of dog in the study. Neither could you define how good a dog would be from it's looks or behaviour. Our training worked with various types of dogs from various backgrounds and of all kinds of temperaments.

Our medical assistance dogs are trained to detect an oncoming episode of life threatening disease such as diabetes, go get a package containing the blood testing kit and place it onto its owner's lap often before the owner is aware of an oncoming hypo.

HYPO (Low Blood Sugar)
Life threatening
Results in diabetic coma/seizure
Emergency paramedic callout
Sudden death
Needs SUGAR to increase blood sugars.

HYPER (High Blood Sugar)
Long term complicated damage to eyes; kidneys; etc
Take insulin to reduce blood sugar levels

Our specialist trained Assistance Dogs provide an early alert to changing glucose levels, prompting clients to take appropriate action.

The dogs provide vital early warning to individuals who suffer brittle/aggressive diabetes and/or poor awareness of dangerously low blood sugar, a condition called hypoglycaemic unawareness.

This early warning given by the dog enables the clients to better regulate harmful side effects.

Preliminary studies of our partnerships suggest that these specialist trained dogs facilitate pronounced reductions in hypos and significantly reduce recipients' requirement for paramedic assistance and hospitalisation. This has potentially significant medical cost savings.

Trained to be highly sensitive to glucose levels, they warn the client when levels deviate from the normal range, and can indicate changes within one or two millimoles of blood sugar.

Normally the dogs are trained to alert to blood sugar levels below 4.5 millimoles per litre and also alert to high blood sugars at the level chosen by the client (normally above 10 to 12 millimoles per litre).

There is a further and very important additional benefit of the placement of a blood sugar detection dog. The increase in client confidence the dogs provide along with their companionship helps save lives, and reduces the tendency to "run blood sugars high" as a method of avoiding hypoglycaemia.

Reduction of prolonged periods of hyperglycaemia (high blood sugars) has a major benefit on the long term health and well-being of individuals with diabetes. High blood sugars are the cause of many of the long-term complications normally associated with diabetes, including sight loss, severe ulcerated wounds, kidney damage, and the amputation of limbs. In some cases the consequences are really horrific, for instance when all limbs are lost. It is clear that preventing such complications is vitally important.

Reducing blood sugars greatly reduces the possibility of these associated side effects. We have early indications that clients with dogs have improved HbA1c (average blood glucose levels). This will have a significant impact on their future health and wellbeing.

Training a blood sugar detection dog requires training in both odour identification and in giving a reliable alert which enables the dog to communicate the changed blood sugar level to the client. All the dogs are also trained to fetch the medical bag/blood testing kit if asked by the client, or when, due to the cognitive confusion caused by low blood sugars, the client does not respond to the alert.

It's incredible when you think about it. We have been using dogs to help man in one form or another for hundreds of years. In recent times they have assisted in discovering drugs, explosives, bodies and all kinds of things that needed a dog's nose to uncover yet we didn't have a clue what their real capacity was.

If you talk to a good handler of a detection dog they will report that after a break they instinctively feel that they should give their dog something easy to find before starting them on their real task.

This is an instinct based on their experience but there is no definitive definition of why or how long it takes a dog to come back to peak performance, or any significant measure of performance.

I am able to reveal some of our study in talks I give and it was tremendous to include some of the data in a presentation I gave at St James Palace in March 2014 to Their Royal Highnesses The Prince of Wales and The Duchess of Cornwall and invited scholars and experts from the medical profession.

The thresholds we achieved and proved really made the scientists sit up and take notice. Many wanted to know how we had achieved these results and I would explain that so much of our success came from the training we gave to the dogs. If you trained in the old fashion way then the dog would respond to its trainer's responses. It is by allowing the dog to take the initiative to tell you when the part was present in a sample that gives it the understanding of what the game is all about and makes the dog all too happy to get the correct result. Guessing brings no reward! Accurate prognoses gains reward and respect so the dog is continually improving its performance.

There has to be a relationship with the dog!

You cannot dictate what you want – the dog has to learn what is expected and be rewarded every time it gets the answer correct, even if the correct answer is a negative result because it cannot detect. The dog that has been trained by the dictatorial orders of it's handler can never gain that understanding as it has been trained to do what the handler tells it and looks for that instruction rather than be able to understand what the task needs.

At long last in 2014 I am accepted by medics and talked to at their level. No longer am I made to feel that they consider me to be that mad woman with the dogs. I really do feel that many, if not most, medics are beginning to get excited about how dogs may be able to help in medical assistance.

The paper we are about to publish in conjunction with Lincoln University and the work we are doing with Addenbrooks will prove that our Medical Assistance Dogs are actually doing the job they were trained for and that we can prove it. We did this work with our first 16 dogs that were out with clients with results published in medical journal PLOS One in 2013.

We have now successfully trained using same methods as the diabetes alert dogs; an Addisonian Crisis Alert dog, Narcolepsy dog, and more recently a dog to alert to an oncoming PoTS attack.

PoTS (Postural Tachycardia Syndrome) is an abnormal response by the autonomic nervous system to becoming upright. There is an abnormally high increase in heart rate and altered blood supply to the brain on standing. It results in a large number of

symptoms, the commonest of which are dizziness, fainting, tiredness and palpitations. There are many causes and, in some cases, no cause can be found although patients can be very disabled by their symptoms, many get better without treatment. However, some patient will have problems over many years.

Source potsuk.org

We have also successfully trained two 'nut' detection dogs for clients who suffer a severe allergic reaction and anaphylaxis from nuts.

The potential for the work of Medical Assistance dogs is truly vast. We are constantly recognising new conditions where our dogs can be of help. This work is ground breaking and the dogs we train are often 'world firsts'.

Our Addisons Crisis detector dog Coco is an example of this. Placed with a lady who has had her adrenal glands removed, Coco alerts to dangerous drops in cortisol which if left unrecognised would result in a life threatening Addisons Crisis which requires immediate hospital admission and often intensive care stays.

Through a simple sniff Coco is able to detect drops in cortisol before they become life threatening allowing the client to take medication at home. It is truly remarkable and I feel humbled and in awe of the ability and dedication of these dogs.

To the dogs it is easy, they detect these changes in us all the time. The training we give simply gives the dog a way of communicating it to us. The result is a happy dog who receives not only a reward of a biscuit or toy but also keeps his owner safe. His potential for the work of medical assistance dogs is truly vast.

The application of the work of Medical Assistance Dogs continues to expand. Our allergen detectors are growing in numbers, the majority of these dogs are nut detectors, warning their owners of the presence of nut contaminate in food or the environment. These dogs provide life-saving alerts preventing anaphylactic shock, an extreme allergic reaction. Again, the dogs love doing this work, to them it is a search game with a reward at the end, but this is a game that saves lives.

As the charity grows we become more aware of the challenges many individuals face in the management of life threatening conditions. Our dogs are only too willing to help if we ask, we simply need to develop our communication with each other.

The charity waiting list is growing rapidly. Often we train rescue dogs or dogs that have been unsuitable for other roles such as gundogs or guide dogs. This work suits a dog that bonds closely with their owner and is a highly inquisitive problem solver.

I have the pleasure of working with happy, fun dogs, the characters of the dog world who previously may well have been labelled naughty or disruptive. It is work that is rewarding for all involved.

If anyone ever raises a concern about dogs that are required to work round the clock, I confidently reassure them that dogs are happy to work for us at any time. By nature a dog would not sleep all through the night as we do, this is simply the dog syncing with human routine. Dogs sleep in short bursts throughout the 24 hour period. They are happy to get up and play during the day or night and will alert to get their reward whenever the change in odour is detected. Humans have always understood this when considering the dog's ability to guard the home. Day or night the dog would raise the alarm to intrusion. This is working in the same way and what a difference it makes.

The potential of this work to save lives is limitless.

What I love most about this work is that the dogs love it so. When trained they look across and say *'Hey, if you wanted to know that how come you never asked before?'*

The charity has a complete no kennels policy. Our dogs are not put into kennels at any time during their training and placement. This includes all our cancer detection dogs who live with trainers or volunteer fosters. To achieve the best results dogs must live alongside us. This establishes the strong relationship needed for our work.

During my work as consultant , I have seen many smart kennels all around the world. I have come to the conclusion the majority of dogs don't like kennels, even when millions are spent on their building and design.Dogs prefer to curl up on the armchair in front of the fire after work, just as we do

Chapter Fifteen
Royal Patronage

All of our Trustees do an excellent job and we are privileged to have them helping us to success. Betsy Duncan-Smith had recovered from breast cancer, joined us and became a Trustee. At our presentation she immediately recognised what a tremendous difference the dog's early diagnosis could have made to her and became an enthusiastic supporter.

She has been a real blessing and her connections opened the door for Medical Detection Dogs to give demonstrations and talks at government and upper echelons of society. She joins me in the belief that Medical Detection Dogs could develop into a charity that could be used by the NHS to conduct first level cancer detection. Urine or even breath samples could be sent to one of our centres for testing and our dogs give a very early warning of Cancer being present in the sample.

Early detection could save many lives and our method of detection using trained dogs at our centres would cost a fraction of NHS costs that are trying to give the same service. NHS could be saved many £millions and many lives could be saved along with vast improvement to the quality of life that early detection and treatment would allow. We are currently demonstrating how much medical assistance dogs save the NHS through their ability to prevent emergency situations, paramedic callouts and hospital admissions.

On a day I will always remember Betsy came through to me and said *'Have you thought of inviting the Duchess of Cornwall to a visit'*

Startled by the question I responded

'Well no! We could do if you thought there was any chance she would be graceful enough to come'.

'You should definitely invite her. I have heard that the Duchess is interested to hear of your work here. I have a feeling that she would be very interested to see what you are accomplishing

We put together a letter of invitation to the Duchess of Cornwall which was delivered to her Private Secretary just before Christmas 2012. When we returned after the New Year a letter came back from the Palace that said The Duchess of Cornwall would be delighted to accept your invitation and would like to visit on 20th February 2013.

We were completely flummoxed! We have no government funding and relied on donations and the kindness of people and organisations that support us thus we housed the whole charity in two small industrial units in Great Horwood, in Buckinghamshire.

We had been negotiating to rent the unit next to ours but that was not yet finalised. The building we wanted was full of spare parts and old engines and frameworks of ancient planes that the owner had been rebuilding. We thus only had one small industrial unit that we had divided up into a training area that was just big enough to house the training carousel and allow the dogs to circle it as they detected the cancerous samples, a minute office, and a kind of foyer area that served to greet people and house our dogs in cages, make a cup of tea or coffee, and do our administration.

The Duchess has been so kind to accept our invitation but how on earth were we to make it such that it is worthy of a Royal visit and she can see all we are trying to do?

We vigorously pursued negotiations for the adjoining industrial unit and finally got the keys 10 days before the actual visit.

When we walked into it all our spirits sagged. The whole unit was filthy black and covered in oil from all the old aircraft parts and engines. How on earth were we to get this ready in time? We only had 10 days!

People appear at the right time and make a huge difference ... my family, each person I have met, every volunteer, every friend and every special dog had their special part to play. Each is a ripple in a pond, together we are becoming a wave.

The solution was the wonderful volunteers, friends and family and my boyfriend Rob the carpenter!

He ripped all the oil-soaked carpet tiles out, put all the new carpet tiles that we had been lucky enough to get donated, he scrubbed and whitewashed the walls and he and all our wonderful volunteers got the whole area including the new unit ready at 2am on the day of the Duchess visit.

The Duchess of Cornwall arrived and I had a dilemma about my role for was I Claire the dog trainer – taking her through all the demonstrations of the dogs working or was I Claire the 'face' of the charity – introducing her to all our employees and many of our volunteers and some of the people who had our Medical Assistance Dogs and could talk about the way the dogs had improved, and in some cases, turned around their lives?

'Claire come quick! The Duchess is arriving at our front door!'

At that moment I was handling urine samples that I was discussing with Rob our dog trainer. Thankfully I remembered to hand them back to Rob as I ran to be at the door to greet the Duchess.

The Duchess is a really lovely lady. I started to introduce her to staff and this became quite hilarious. We had rehearsed the line-up and that each of the ladies would give a little curtsy and if spoken to would start their answer with *'Good morning your Royal Highness'*

In the event most of them reacted totally unpredictably and completely out of character as if overwhelmed by the Royal presence.

The first girl was holding a puppy and the Duchess is clearly fond of dogs, and this went well. The Duchess patted 'Charlie' – the 8 week old puppy who has gone on to be the first dog trained to give alerts to a client who is suffering from the condition 'POTS' – a world first!

The second girl shouted *'Hello'* and did a unique rendering of a curtsy. The third girl was my sister Simone, who curtsied perfectly but then got flummoxed on what to say when the Duchess asked her *'How did you hear about the charity?'*

Simone didn't know whether to admit that she was my sister and that she had been here from the start and that we had started the charity together or to think up some other answer. I could see this all going through Simone's mind and all she could do was to stare and say nothing. I think the Duchess put the reaction down to nervousness on the part of Simone and moved onto the next in line who I had introduced as Kimberley. Before she could say a word she was greeted with staring eyes and a shouted *'I'm a Type One Diabetic!'*

The Duchess ignored the lack of protocol in the greeting but

kindly said *'Oh, you are a diabetic, I'm Patron of JRF* (Juvenile Diabetes Association)' strangely Kimberley had never heard of JRF so replied *'Hello, I'm a type one diabetic'*

What the Duchess must have thought by now I dread to think but I found it hard to suppress my giggles and the Duchess seemed far too nice a person to comment.

I then walked her into the demonstration room and introduced her to all the Trustees and top Oncologists and Doctors who were present including Professor Karol Sikora who had helped me so much in our early days and Alan Makepeace..

I talked through what Daisy was about to do and you could see that the Duchess was immediately comfortable with all dogs.

Daisy was to work on one type of Cancer which she did beautifully. The Duchess was watching and discussing with the Doctors and Oncologists the potential for Cancer Detection through the work of our dogs.

We then took her round to the new unit where volunteers, helpers and many of those with our Medical Assistance Dogs were gathered along with their dogs. She met some of our clients and some of those who had kindly provided finance to the charity. She then gave a little speech saying how greatly impressed she was to have seen the work being done by the charity and how delighted she was to have been invited.

As she left she said quietly to me *'I'm going to tell my husband about you!'*

It had been a wonderful visit. Photos of her visits made the National and Local press and was a terrific boost to our publicity and our credibility.

It was the first real indication to me that the charity I had pictured in my head of hundreds of dogs in their red jackets all providing Medical Detection or Medical Assistance had nearly arrived – or at least the first stages of it had come together. All the people who had been there with me during all or part of this journey were there together on that day. It was a dream come true.

Claire Guest
"Listened to Daisy"

Following her visit in March 2013 we started to receive invitation to give talks to potential benefactors who supported worthwhile projects and secured a 3 year grant from one which was heaven sent as it gave us the financial security we had never previously enjoyed and financed most of what we wanted to do for the next 3 years.

Another huge boost came when the Executors of the Will of a very wealthy lady named Sylvia who had passed away followed her instructions as to the type of charity she wished to sponsor after her death. They awarded us enough money to enable us to completely repay the mortgage on number 3 Millfield at Great Horwood and enabled us to buy the adjoining units and the paddock on which we exercise and train the dogs.

We were kept in touch with the Duchess's private secretary and she advised that the Duchess had indeed spoken to her husband about us and asked would I meet with one of Prince Charles' private secretaries. I of course agreed.

The secretary had a number of questions for me advised His Royal Highness the Prince of Wales was very interested in our charity. He added *'The Prince wishes to offer you the opportunity of an event. He is very interested in your work and would like to help the charity move forward. He wonders if it might help if you had a small engagement at St James Palace?'*

You could imagine my excitement!

After years of trying to get acceptance of our work and the results we were producing I have the approval of His Royal Highness Prince Charles, the Prince of Wales and he is offering me an event at his Royal Palace.

I managed to control my voice

'Oh I think we could manage that very nicely.'

We continued in dialogue with the secretary and it transpired that His Royal Highness was willing to send out the invitations from his office rather than us doing so thus practically guaranteeing that all the top medical people and those from leading cancer charities that had so often ignored me in the past would be in attendance. An invitation to them from the Prince of Wales and the Duchess of Cornwall would not be ignored!

Betsy and I were invited to visit St James Palace to plan how the demonstration would go.

The private secretary continued to calmly make the most gracious offers of help and not once did his tone reveal that he knew how excited we were by this invitation.

'The rooms at Clarence House are a little small to accommodate your Cancer Detection Carousel and a 50 strong audience and we are concerned that they would not be big enough.' He said, *'We thought perhaps we should be in St James's Palace; perhaps the Throne Room?'*

He showed us into the magnificent Throne Room.

Needless to say it was an incredible room of such opulence that it took my breath away. Red carpeted an eloquence of gold that left Betsy and I goggle-eyed.

'This would be perfect' was the only response I could give.

From then we were in constant contact as we set up the event. The Prince of Wales' private secretary was incredibly kind to us. We worked with a number of secretaries and officials at the Palace particularly the Duchess's. They were all delightful, helpful, enthusiastic and supportive.

'Don't get worried about anything. It will all go splendidly. Prince Charles and the Duchess of Cornwall are determined to do all they can to help your charity to be successful. They are thrilled to have you here.'

During that time we were planning the event I wondered whether it would be acceptable to ask the Duchess of Cornwall to be our Patron.

She replied *'I think it would be a good idea to ask her now'*

When we got back to Great Horwood we drafted a letter.

We got a nice reply back saying that she would consider our request. What this meant was that along with other considerations we were to be investigated to ensure that there was no underlying reasons that should prevent her accepting the role if she so wished.

Someone from Imperial College was appointed to do all the due diligence on our worth without our knowledge. When we finally got to meet him he said he was extremely impressed with our charity and could not find a single thing detrimental. He advised that he had been very happy to assure the Duchess that we were worthy of her Patronage.

We got the news of her acceptance of the role of Patron of Medical Detection Dogs on the day of our event at St James Palace.

We were allowed to invite guests to the event and I decided to concentrate where I felt we could get the greatest beneficial result. I settled on specialists from cancer treatment and research. It was a very scientific audience.

I didn't learn my speech off by heart but I had all my bullet points in my head. I was ready the night before when ITV came through at 11 o'clock at night wanting our Ambassador Lesley Nicol (aka Mrs Patmore in Downton Abbey) and a dog on the sofa in the Breakfast Show the following morning.

With all we had going on it was tempting to ignore them and search for another date but they were insistent and the publicity would do the charity the world of good. The problem was I needed to spend the next couple of hours organising the ITV interview and to make matters worse ITV were on again at one o'clock in the morning asking if I could send them video footage of Daisy working.

I got very little sleep before the biggest possible event in my charity's life.

Simone joined Lesley to the ITV studios with the dog as a standby in case of problems but it all went well and she came onto St James Palace, arriving before the rest of us. She was worried that her dog had not had the opportunity to go to the toilet at the ITV studios and asked an assistant if there was a door anywhere she could take her dog into a grassy area. She assured him she had poop scoops with her and he let her out into the garden. All of which was unknown to his Royal Highness and the Duchess.

It was rumoured that the Duchess caught sight of a strange dog in the garden, it was a Poodle! Where had it come from? - and it was doing a poo!

Thankfully Simone then came into sight and poop scooped and it was realised it was one of the Medical Detection dogs so all was well.

Prince Charles and the Duchess of Cornwall were hosts and the initial presentation had gone perfectly.

Whilst explaining what we were about to demonstrate it was clear to see the complete non-believers and those antagonistic towards the whole concept of dogs sniffing out cancer by their body language.

There were top scientists, top cancer specialists, top people from the cancer charities, top oncologists, government advisors and people with influence in financial donations and supporters of charities in the audience.

I was able to include a number of facts and statistics from the paper we were about to release and I could see a change from many of them that indicated that they had never before studied earlier papers we had released or the data we had available.

I screened the figures on PowerPoint. They revealed that Daisy had by that time screened more than 6,000 samples and had recorded 93% accuracy in detecting cancer!

From their reaction I guessed this was way beyond the highest achievement of the Cancer departments of most if not all the audience.

They were then able to see Daisy working and as is often the case it was the demonstration from the dogs that convinces them.

We had decided to take a bit of a risk and work on 3 different kinds of cancer and use 3 different dogs. It was the first time the carousel had been out of the Training Centre so we had no guarantee of performance of dogs or equipment but if it all worked – dogs and equipment; and Rob and I were confident it would - then the audience could never again throw doubts up about our work.

Amongst the Cancers we were going to include one very, very early sample of Renal Cancer which is terribly difficult and often impossible to detect by any known means.

We trusted the dogs. We started with Lucy working on Bladder Cancer. Lucy got it spot on first time around the carousel; hesitated second time but got the next Bladder Cancer sample.

'Now we are going to introduce Daisy who will be looking to detect a very early Renal Cancer sample! Daisy has been trained on Prostate and Bladder Cancer but we have obtained a very early Renal Cancer sample and we will see if Daisy can detect it!'

Daisy got to work at the carousel and was so quick and efficient and as soon as she was round the carousel to where the sample was she immediately sat looking straight at it.

You could hear the gasps of disbelief coming from so many of the audience who had not believed a dog could be so efficient, fast and as effective as the demonstration they had just watched.

We then used Ulrich to work on Prostate Cancer.

They were all so effective that we were told afterwards that some of the audience including her Royal Highness the Duchess of Cornwall had tears in their eyes at the end of the demonstrations.

They realised how many lives these dogs could save and how simple it was without any invasive investigative surgery. Bill Baily the well-known comedian and advocate of improved Prostate Cancer screening was also very moved by the demonstration.

The timing had been spot on. The dogs performed exactly right and everything came out perfectly. It was terrifically well received. The whole event had gone extremely well.

It was wonderful to see the Duchess talking to

some of the dogs of our clients who were there to talk about the immense improvement to their quality of life that the dogs had brought. She chatted to our clients so naturally and with great interest as she did with me and our supporters. The Duchess could immediately understand just how these dog skills can be used to benefit people who suffer from all kinds of debilitating or life threatening diseases.

Amongst the audience was Professor Hardev Pandha - a world renowned specialist in markers for Prostate Cancer. At the reception at Clarence House that followed he asked

'Would you like to come down and meet the team at the Department of bio-science for medicine in the Cancer department at the University of Surrey?'

'I would love to.'

I received an invite a week or so later and went to visit them in Surrey.

Immediately what struck me as I walked into the department was that I was being treated on equal terms as all the specialists. This was the first time this had ever happened to me.

I was introduced as Claire Guest who is in Cancer Research. Previously I had always been disparaged as some mad woman with dogs. We had a meeting to see what areas we could work together.

They showed me all around the department looking at cancer cells and the research they were doing on them and responded to any questions I had. They treated me as an equal.

Being treated in this way was so refreshing and stimulating.

A couple of weeks later I got a call from Anjum Iqbal. If Medical Detection Dogs could get clearance on our Ethics Proposal that was under consideration then he could share cancer samples that had been donated over the years by cancer patients for use in research.

'I would like you to use these samples as you do with the dogs and we can use the results of your work alongside the work we do here on the same samples'

He added *'Would you like to have a member of your staff in our department so that we can investigate the best way of combining our research? They can also collect samples on a daily basis and send them back to you so that you have a regular supply for your work'*

Our work with dogs and Medical Detection Dogs is accepted at last!

What a day it had been at the Palace.

So many people had come up to me to say that they had not believed in our work until then. So many had previously doubted or even ignored our work and ignored all our invitations to come and see our dogs working but now they were offering to do anything they could to help.

It had been a fabulous day!

In addition to all the above we had been given the news that the Duchess of Cornwall had kindly agreed to become Patron of Medical Detection Dogs.

***

DAISY *(an extract from a letter by Dr Claire Guest)*
Daisy is a truly wonderful dog. She has a beautiful gentle temperament which shines through her eyes. During the past 10 years she has lived with me and worked as a cancer detection dog. Due to her work the charity has been able to make discoveries about human cancer that will change the diagnosis for humans all over the world. This knowledge could potentially save thousands of lives.

I know that Wendy has told you that she was a leading part of the team, the study which was published in the Journal of Cancer Biomarkers in 2011. This work has provided scientists with information which is speeding the development of electronic systems for the diagnosis of human cancer bio-markers. In the shorter term Daisy is invaluable for second line screening as part of a prostate cancer study which the charity is currently undergoing. I attach graphical information that shows Daisy's current reliability [93% accuracy]of detection for over 6000 patients.

Along with Tangle a spaniel who lives with Daisy at home with me, Daisy has been integral in the formation of the charity Medical Detection Dogs. The charity would not have achieved what it has to date without her.

In addition to the above I owe my life to her. She was by my side at all times following a period of deep depression following a traumatic divorce and then drew my attention to a very deep seated breast cancer. My treatment which included surgery, lymph node removal and intensive radiotherapy removed the cancer but my consultants were in agreement that due to the deep nature of the cancer without Daisy's warning my prognosis would have been very different.

The consultants were so taken with Daisy's story and the work of the charity that we have now started the first robust proof of principle trial investigating the potential of dogs to detect human breast cancer from a breath sample. My surgeon is the Principle Investigator in the study.

There is so much more that can be said. Daisy has a gentleness of spirit that touches everyone who has contact with her. I am privileged to own and work with her.
Claire Guest

Daisy was awarded the
'BLUE CROSS MEDAL" in 2014
(the medal was previously awarded in 2007)

Claire Guest
"Listened to Daisy"

Please go to
www.medicaldetectiondogs.org.uk
to learn more about the wonderful work
the charity is currently achieving.

Claire Guest
"Listened to Daisy"

Our publisher;**TwigBooks** specialises in **Stories of Interest**.
www.twigbooks.com gives details but 3 more you may enjoy are -

Poverty to Peaches by **Terry Gasking** – ISBN 9781907953 545
Told and lived with ever-present humour it is a book the reader finds difficult to put down.   From absolute poverty, bombed, evacuated, the bombed out houses and horse drawn barges of the East-end of London as his playground with only a single candle for heat and light to complete his homework, dogged by ill-health, the author surmounted many severe problems in life. He bounced back from events that could flatten life prospects of many to become a leading financial consultant working to 'turn around' companies in many parts of the world. This is an eventful life-story full of fun and tragedies and reveals one man's determination to overcome all that life could throw at him.

Stanley Orman "An Uncivil Civil Servant" ISBN 978-1-907953-569
From a council house in London's East End, evacuated during World War II, Grammar School, College, International Athletics, Scholar, Scientist, Administrator, Diplomat. This is a most extraordinary story of an extraordinary man who played a hugely significant role in ensuring the defence of the U.K. and the U.S.A from the threat of nuclear destruction.

Father Away by **Philip Anderson** – ISBN 9781907973 590
Memoir of a Quest - is a story about a search for a missing father, a figure in the shadow. The tale evokes the atmosphere of Fifties and Sixties in rural England told by a boy of mixed race with an absent father. It describes the desire to know what has become of the father who had departed the scene in dramatic circumstances. Philip, at his mother's behest, begins a long and tortuous search based on very little data. Background to the narrative is provided by the intercultural context of the author's adult life in Germany and ongoing research into an Indian background shrouded in mystery.
This is also about the yearnings and ambiguities which people in search of a lost relative – especially a parent – experience in various forms. It is a tale of false leads, cul-de-sacs and dashed hopes, but one which ultimately leads to a satisfying resolution.

For more information on the books we publish or to download into
your IPad, Mobile device or computer please go to –
www.twigbooks.com

Claire Guest
"Listened to Daisy"

DAISY

This beautiful portrait is included with the kind permission of
Bridget Wood

Claire Guest
"Listened to Daisy"

Claire Guest
"Listened to Daisy"

Lightning Source UK Ltd.
Milton Keynes UK
UKOW07f1221181114

241792UK00015B/148/P

9 781907 953576